ESSENTIAL
AFRICAN AMERICAN
WISDOM

ESSENTIAL
AFRICAN AMERICAN
WISDOM

Edited by
Carol Kelly-Gangi

FALL RIVER PRESS

To John and Emily with love.

Book design by Lundquist Design, New York

Fall River Press
387 Park Avenue
New York, NY 10016

ISBN: 978-1-4351-1812-6

Printed and bound in the United States of America

10 9 8 7 6 5 4 3 2 1

 The pages of this book contain 30% recycled fiber

Contents

Introduction

THE FIRST AFRICAN SLAVES were brought to American shores in the early 1600s. By the time of the 1860 census, the number of African American slaves had reached four million. Clearly, the contributions of African Americans to the fledgling nation were immense. Yet, it was not until 1926 that there was any official recognition of African American history. Dr. Carter G. Woodson, the Harvard-educated scholar and son of former slaves, is responsible for what began as "Negro History Week," which he initiated in an effort to bring a national spotlight to the contributions of African Americans. Up until that point, African Americans had been virtually ignored in U.S. history books, or if they were included at all, it was with a negative and racist slant. In 1976, Woodson's commemoration was extended to a month and designated as Black History Month.

Though it is not possible to pigeonhole the importance of African American history into the confines of a single month, the larger issue may be, as Morgan Freeman has stated, Black history *is* American history. To help illustrate that point,

Essential African American Wisdom gathers more than 350 quotations from an extraordinary group of men and women who have shaped our country in immeasurable ways from colonial times up to the present day. In an effort to capture a rich array of African American voices, there are contributors from many walks of life. There are excerpts from scholars and writers; politicians and religious leaders; sports figures and entertainers; artists and educators.

While there are some universal themes that inevitably emerge, such as the struggle for equality; the enduring obstacle of racism; the quest for knowledge; and the love of family; the excerpts are as individual as the contributors themselves. In the selections that follow, Frederick Douglass exposes the hypocrisy of Independence Day amidst the horrors of slavery; Harriet Tubman vividly recalls her first moments of freedom; and Rosa Parks reflects on her contribution to the Civil Rights Movement. Then there's Louis Armstrong who wryly sums up the meaning of jazz; Alice Walker's take on the secret to a happy marriage; and Colin Powell's challenge to students to find strength in diversity. In a dialogue that ebbs and flows across the boundaries of time and place, the contributors also exchange views on such subjects as the meaning of love; the role of religion; the need for reform; and the pitfalls of success.

With a richness and eloquence that speaks to the human condition first and foremost, *Essential African American Wisdom* is also a living testament to the African American men and women who continue to leave an indelible mark on our nation's history in every area of endeavor.

— Carol Kelly-Gangi
Rumson, New Jersey, 2009

Slavery and Its Legacy

A tale of woe with tones loud, long, and deep; they breathed the prayers and complaints of souls boiling over with the bitterest anguish. Every tone was a testimony against slavery, and a prayer to God for deliverance from chains.

— Frederick Douglass, *Life and Times of
Frederick Douglass*, 1881

For every hundred of us who survived the terrible journey across the Atlantic . . . four hundred of us perished. During three hundred years—the seventeenth, eighteenth, and nineteenth centuries—more than 100,000,000 of us were torn from our African homes.

— Richard Wright, *12 Million Black Voices*, 1941

Because God is not dead slavery can only end in blood.

> — Sojourner Truth, *Narrative of the Life of Sojourner Truth*, 1850

The rule on the place was: Wake up the slaves at daylight, begin work when they can see, and quit work when they can't see.

> — Peter Clifton, South Carolina, from slave narratives compiled by WPA, 1930s

Slavery is terrible for men; but it is far more terrible for women. Super-added to the burdens common to all, they have wrongs and sufferings and mortifications peculiarly their own.

> — Harriet Jacobs, *Incidents in the Life of a Slave Girl*, 1861

For God's sake, don't be catch with pencil and paper. That was a major crime. You might as well had killed your marster or missus.

> — Elijah Green, South Carolina, from slave narratives compiled by WPA, 1930s

You never knew what it is to be a slave; to be entirely unprotected by law or custom; to have the laws reduce you to the condition of a chattel, entirely subject to the will of another. You never exhausted your ingenuity in avoiding the snares, and eluding the power of a hated tyrant; you never shuddered at the sound of his footsteps, and trembled within hearing of his voice.

— Harriet Jacobs, *Incidents in the Life of a Slave Girl*, 1861

I don't know how we live, yet we is.

— Ann Perry, South Carolina, from slave narratives compiled by WPA, 1930s

You have seen how a man was made a slave; you shall see how a slave was made a man.

— Frederick Douglass, *Narrative of the Life of Frederick Douglass*, 1845

I could never be of any service to anyone as a slave.

— Nat Turner, *Confessions of Nat Turner*, November 5, 1831

No man can put a chain about the ankle of his fellow man without at last finding the other end fastened about his own neck.

— Frederick Douglass, speech at Civil Rights Mass Meeting, Washington, D.C., October 22, 1883

What, to the American slave, is your Fourth of July? I answer: A day that reveals to him, more than all other days in the year, the gross injustice and cruelty to which he is the constant victim. To him your celebration is a sham.

— Frederick Douglass, speech at Rochester, New York, July 4, 1852

When I found I had crossed that line, [her first escape from slavery in 1845] I looked at my hands to see if I was the same person. There was such a glory over everything.

— Harriet Tubman, to her biographer, Sarah H. Bradford, c. 1868

It has been a matter of deep interest to me to note the number of people who have come to shake hands with me after an address, who say that this is the first time they have ever called a Negro "Mister."

— Booker T. Washington, *Up from Slavery: An Autobiography*, 1901

Whenever and wherever men have been oppressed and enslaved, their oppressors and enslavers have, in every instance, found a warrant in the character of the victim.

— Frederick Douglass, "The Proclamation and a Negro Army," speech, New York City, February 6, 1863

The first excuse given to the civilized world for the murder of unoffending Negroes was the necessity of the white man to repress and stamp out "race riots." . . . It was always a remarkable feature in these insurrections and riots that only Negroes were killed during the rioting, and that all the white men escaped unharmed.

— Ida B. Wells, *A Red Record*, 1895

They can put him in a smoking car or baggage car—take him or leave him at a railroad station, exclude him from inns, drive him from all places of amusement or instruction without the least fear of the national government interfering for the protection of his liberty.

— Frederick Douglass, c. 1875

In 1896, the Supreme Court upheld segregation in its separate but equal doctrine set forth in *Plessy v. Ferguson*.

— John Hope Franklin, *From Slavery
to Freedom*, 1947

Separation is nothing but a form of slavery covered up with certain niceties of complexity.

— Martin Luther King, Jr., *Stride Toward
Freedom*, 1958

The very nature of segregation was demeaning, and its effect upon its victim was deadening.

— Benjamin Davis, Jr., *Benjamin Davis, Jr.:
An Autobiography*, 1991

We have been sentenced to die for something we ain't never done. Us poor boys been sentenced to burn up on the electric chair for the reason that we is workers—and the color of our skin is black.

> — Andy and Leroy Wright, Olen Montgomery, Ozie Powell, Charlie Weems, Clarence Norris, Haywood Patterson, Eugene Williams, and Willie Roberson; collectively known as "The Scottsboro Boys," quoted in *The Negro Worker*, May 1932

The Black woman in the South who raises sons, grandsons, and nephews had her heartstrings tied to a hanging noose.

> — Maya Angelou, *I Know Why the Caged Bird Sings*, 1969

Southern trees bear a strange fruit,
Blood on the leaves and blood at the root,
Black bodies swinging in the Southern breeze,
Strange fruit hanging from the poplar trees.

> — Billie Holiday, "Strange Fruit," 1939

If we must die, let it not be like hogs
Hunted and penned in an inglorious spot.

— Claude McKay, *If We Must Die*, 1919

But I don't know how to fight. All I know how to do is stay alive.

— Alice Walker, *The Color Purple*, 1982

The purpose of evil was to survive it.

— Toni Morrison, *Sula*, 1973

Only base men and oppressors can rejoice in a triumph of injustice over the weak and defenseless, for weakness ought itself to protect from assaults of pride, prejudice, and power.

— Frederick Douglass, *Life and Times of Frederick Douglass*, 1881

I imagine one of the reasons people cling to their hates so stubbornly is because they sense, once hate is gone, they will be forced to deal with pain.

— James Baldwin, *Notes of a Native Son*, 1955

Oppression does not always crush the spirit of progress. Men will achieve in spite of it.

— Carter G. Woodson, *Negro Makers of History*, 1928

Freedom, Equality, and Justice

The whole history of the progress of human liberty shows that all concessions yet made to her august claims have been born of earnest struggle. . . . If there is no struggle, there is no progress. Those who profess to favor freedom, and yet deprecate agitation, are men who want crops without plowing up the ground, they want rain without thunder and lightning. They want the ocean without the awful roar of its many waters.

— Frederick Douglass, speech, Canandaigua,
New York, August 3, 1857

Freedom is never given; it is won.

— A. Phillip Randolph, speech to the Second
National Negro Congress, 1937

The cost of liberty is less than the price of repression.

— W. E. B. Du Bois, *John Brown*, 1909

I had reasoned this out in my mind, there was two things I had a right to, liberty and death. If I could not have one, I would have the other, for no man should take me alive.

— Harriet Tubman, to her biographer,
Sarah H. Bradford, c. 1868

We will be ourselves and free, or die in the attempt. Harriet Tubman was not our great-grandmother for nothing.

— Alice Walker, *You Can't Keep a
Good Woman Down*, 1981

You profess to believe that "of one blood God made all nations of men to dwell on the face of all the earth"—and hath commanded all men, everywhere, to love one another—yet you notoriously hate (and glory in your hatred!) all men whose skins are not colored like your own!

— Frederick Douglass, speech, Rochester,
New York, July 4, 1852

What does the Negro want? His answer is very simple. He wants only what all other Americans want. He wants opportunity to make real what the Declaration of Independence and the Constitution and the Bill of Rights say, what the Four Freedoms establish. While he knows these ideals are open to no man completely, he wants only his equal chance to obtain them.

— Mary McLeod Bethune, "Certain Unalienable Rights," *What the Negro Wants*, 1944, edited by Rayford W. Logan

Words like "freedom," "justice," "democracy," are not common concepts; on the contrary, they are rare. People are not born knowing what these are. It takes enormous and, above all, individual effort to arrive at the respect for other people that these words imply.

— James Baldwin, "The Crusade of Indignation," *The Nation*, July 7, 1956

Well, charity ain't justice. Charity is beautiful, but you ain't got to be charitable to me if I already got justice. If I already got a sense of participation, you ain't got to be charitable to me. Just treat me right everyday.

— Michael Eric Dyson, speech, Washington D.C., 2005

My mother believed in freedom and equality even though we didn't know it for reality during our life in Alabama.

> — Rosa Parks, *I Dream a World*, edited by
> Barbara Summers and Yvonne Easton, 1999

We cannot be equal with the master until we own what the master owns. We cannot be equal with the master until we have the freedom the master enjoys. We cannot be equal with the master until we have the education the master has. Then, we can say, "Master, recognize us as your equal."

> — Elijah Muhammad, *Message to the
> Black Man in America*, 1965

You learn about equality in history and civics, but you find out life is not really like that.

> — Arthur Ashe, widely attributed

When equal performance does not result in equal advancement, then something is wrong with the system, and our leaders have an obligation to fix it. If a history of discrimination has made it difficult for certain Americans to meet standards, it is only fair to provide temporary means to help them catch up and compete on equal terms. Affirmative action in the best sense promotes equal consideration, not reverse discrimination.

> — Colin Powell, *My American Journey*, by Colin Powell with Joseph E. Persico, 1995

Where justice is denied, where poverty is enforced, where ignorance prevails, and where any one class is made to feel that society is in an organized conspiracy to oppress, rob, and degrade them, neither persons nor property will be safe.

> — Frederick Douglass, speech on the 23rd anniversary of Emancipation in the District of Columbia, Washington, D.C., April 1885

The only protection against injustice in man is power— physical, financial, and scientific.

> — Marcus Garvey, *Philosophy and Opinions of Marcus Garvey*, volume 2, compiled by Amy Jacques Garvey, 1925

To demand freedom is to demand justice. When there is no justice in the land, a man's freedom is threatened. Freedom and justice are interdependent. When a man has no protection under the law it is difficult for him to make others recognize him.

— James Cone, *Black Theology and Black Power*, 1969

Ignorance, allied with power, is the most ferocious enemy justice can have.

— James Baldwin, *No Name in the Street*, 1972

I felt that one had better die fighting against injustice than to die like a dog or rat in a trap. I had already determined to sell my life as dearly as possible if attacked. I felt if I could take one lyncher with me, this would even up the score a little bit.

— Ida B. Wells, *Crusade for Justice: The Autobiography of Ida B. Wells*, edited by Alfreda M. Duster (published posthumously, 1970)

"We, the people." It is a very eloquent beginning. But when that document [the Preamble to the U.S. Constitution] was completed on the seventeenth of September in 1787 I was not included in that "We, the people." I felt somehow for many years that George Washington and Alexander Hamilton, just left me out by mistake. But through the process of amendment, interpretation and court decision I have finally been included in "We, the people."

— Barbara C. Jordan, statement made
before the House Committee on the Judiciary,
July 25, 1974

If one really wishes to know how justice is administered in a country, one does not question the policemen, the lawyers, the judges, or the protected members of the middle class. One goes to the unprotected—those, precisely, who need the law's protection most!—and listens to their testimony.

— James Baldwin, *No Name in the Street*, 1972

I'll tell you who is the greatest agitator in this country . . . the greatest agitator is injustice.

— William Pickens, *Children of the Slaves*, 1919

We call on America to sow the seeds of social justice and racial equality that it may reap a harvest of righteousness and freedom for all.

— John E. Jacob, speech, New Orleans,
July 31, 1983

Social change rarely comes about through the efforts of the disenfranchised. The middle class creates social revolutions. When a group of people are disproportionately concerned with daily survival, it's not likely that they have the resources to go to Washington and march.

— Faye Wattleton, *Time*, December 11, 1989

I see that the path of progress has never taken a straight line, but has always been a zigzag course amid the conflicting forces of right and wrong, truth and error, justice and injustice, cruelty and mercy.

— Kelly Miller, *Out of the House of Bondage*, 1914

25

Race and Racism

The relation subsisting between the white and colored people of this country is the great, paramount, imperative, and all-commanding question for this age and nation to solve.

— Frederick Douglass, speech at the Church
of the Puritans, New York City, May 1863

In all the relations of life and death, we are met by the color line.

— Frederick Douglass, speech at the Convention
of Colored Men, Louisville, Kentucky,
September 24, 1883

I am not tragically colored. There is no great sorrow dammed up in my soul, nor lurking behind my eyes. . . . Even in the helter-skelter skirmish that is my life, I have seen that the world is to the strong regardless of a little pigmentation more or less. No, I do not weep at the world—I am too busy sharpening my oyster knife.

— Zora Neale Hurston, "How It Feels
to Be Colored Me," 1928

Not to know what one's race has done in former times is to continue always a child.

— Carter G. Woodson, *The Story of
the Negro Retold*, 1955

I am an invisible man. . . . I am a man of substance, of flesh and bone, fiber and liquids—and I might even be said to possess a mind. I am invisible, understand, simply because people refuse to see me.

— Ralph Ellison, *Invisible Man*, 1952

Goddammit, look! We live here and they live there. We black and they white. They got things and we ain't. They do things and we can't. It's just like living in jail.

— Richard Wright, *Native Son*, 1940

If you're born in America with a black skin, you're born in prison.

— Malcolm X, June 1963

Negro blood is sure powerful—because just one drop of black blood makes a colored man. One drop—you are a Negro! . . . Black is powerful.

— Langston Hughes, c. 1953

Being black is the greatest burden I've had to bear.

— Arthur Ashe, *Days of Grace*, by Arthur Ashe and Arnold Rampersad, 1993

The children of these disillusioned colored pioneers inherited the total lot of their parents—the disappointments, the anger. To add to their misery, they had little hope of deliverance. For where does one run to when he's already in the promised land?

> — Claude Brown, *Manchild in the Promised Land*, 1965

It is the duty of the younger Negro artist . . . to change through the force of his art that old whispering "I want to be white, " hidden in the aspirations of his people, to "Why should I want to be white? I am a Negro—and beautiful!"

> — Langston Hughes, "The Negro Artist and the Racial Mountain," *The Nation*, June 23, 1926

The fact that white people readily and proudly call themselves "white," glorify all that is white, and whitewash all that is glorified, becomes unnatural and bigoted in its intent only when these same whites deny persons of African heritage who are Black the natural and inalienable right to readily—proudly—call themselves "black," glorify all that is black, and blackwash all that is glorified.

> — Abbey Lincoln, "Who Will Revere the Black Woman?" *Negro Digest*, September 1966

A little black girl yearns for the blue eyes of a little white girl, and the horror at the heart of her yearning is exceeded only by the evil of fulfillment.

— Toni Morrison, *The Bluest Eye*, 1970

Not that I'd want to forget being black, but I would love to walk through life without the anxiety of being prejudged and pigeonholed on the basis of my race.

— Rita Dove, *Callaloo*, Spring 1991

I have learned that color alone is not sufficient reason for conflict or for connection. Color does not inevitably bond, just as it must not inevitably separate. There is nothing inherently, automatically bonding about skin color. Skin is only tissue, pigment, surface. Skin is not identity.

— James Earl Jones, *Voices and Silences*, 1993

Racism is a contempt for life, an arrogant assertion that one race is the center of value and object of devotion, before which other races must kneel in submission.

— Martin Luther King, Jr., *Where Do We Go From Here?*, 1958

Racism keeps people who are being managed from finding out the truth through contact with each other.

— Shirley Chisholm, *Unbought and Unbossed*, 1970

I am a person who has never completely escaped from the scars of my childhood. Racism, which leaves a shadow on one's sense of accomplishment, can make one feel like a perpetual outsider.

— Alvin Ailey, quoted in *The African American Century*, by Henry Louis Gates, Jr., and Cornel West, 2000

Racism is easy to see, hard to prove, impossible to deny.

— Anonymous

As long as the colored man look to white folks to put the crown on what he say . . . as long as he looks to white folks for approval . . . then he ain't never gonna find out who he is and what he's about.

— August Wilson, Jr., *Ma Rainey's Black Bottom*, 1984

I recall my mother telling me that just because you are black, you are going to have to work 100 percent more than everyone else just to be considered equal. That is unfair, but it is the reality of the situation.

— Vanessa Williams, *Ebony*, April 1990

I never doubted my ability, but when you hear all your life you're inferior, it makes you wonder if the other guys have something you've never seen before. If they do, I'm still looking for it.

— Hank Aaron, *I Had a Hammer*, by Hank Aaron with Lonnie Wheeler, 1992

I've always maintained that black people and women suffer from a presumption of incompetence. The burdens of proof are different. It just gets so tiresome.

— Carol Mosely-Braun, as quoted in the
Chicago Tribune

Racism and sexism must never be an excuse for not doing your best.

— Arthur Ashe, from a letter to his daughter
in *Days of Grace*, by Arthur Ashe and
Arnold Rampersad, 1993

As long as you keep a person down, some part of you has to be down there to hold him down, so it means you cannot soar as you otherwise might.

— Marian Anderson, interview on CBS-TV,
December 30, 1957

Black people have always been America's wilderness in search of a promised land.

— Cornel West, *Race Matters*, 1993

All of us are part white, and all of y'all are part colored.

— Ralph Ellison, address, Harvard University, 1973

I think if you're an interracial child and you're strong enough to live "I'm neither black nor white but in the middle," then, more power. But I *needed* to make a choice and feel part of this culture. I feel a lot of pride in being a black woman.

— Halle Berry, *Ebony*, April 1993

I remember my parents explaining to me that racism would be a part of my life. They told me to always be aware of who was in front of me or in back of me and to always remain prepared. These lessons even extended into school. My parents talked to me about being better than everyone else. . . . I think that's the right approach, no matter what color you are and whether you think you're going to be treated fairly or unfairly. I always try to be better than everyone at anything I do.

— Derek Jeter, *The Life You Imagine*, by Derek Jeter with Jack Curry, 2000

I think for a number of people, the idea of a secure, confident male who is black is disturbing, and possibly unnerving.

— Bryant Gumbel, *Mirabella*, February 1993

When I say, "Don't think of me as Black or White," all I'm saying is, view me as a person. I know my race.

— Michael Jordan, *GQ*, March 1989

If I weren't earning more than $3 million a year to dunk a basketball, most people on the street would run in the other direction if they saw me coming.

— Charles Barkley, *Talkin' Trash*, by Kevin Nelson, 1993

I've learned that I must find positive outlets for anger or it will destroy me. There is a certain anger: it reaches such intensity that to express it fully would require homicidal rage—self-destructive, destroy-the-world rage—and its flame burns because the world is so unjust. I have to try to find a way to channel that anger to the positive, and the highest positive is forgiveness.

— Sidney Poitier, *The Measure of A Man: A Spiritual Autobiography*, 2000

Black people have never had the power to enforce racism, and so this is something that white America is going to have to work out themselves. If they decide they want to stop it, curtail it, or do the right thing . . . then it will be done, but not until then.

> — Spike Lee, quoted in *Home Movie Companion*, by Roger Ebert, 1990

To think clearly about race, then, requires us to see the world on a split screen—to maintain in our sights the kind of America that we want while looking squarely at America as it is, to acknowledge the sins of our past and the challenges of the present without becoming trapped in cynicism or despair. I have witnessed a profound shift in race relations in my lifetime. I have felt it as surely as one feels a change in the temperature. When I hear some in the black community deny those changes, I think it not only dishonors those who struggled on our behalf but also robs us of our agency to complete the work they began. But as much as I insist that things have gotten better, I am mindful of this truth as well: Better isn't good enough.

> — Barack Obama, *The Audacity of Hope*, 2006

The Civil Rights Movement

The dark world is going to submit to its present treatment just as long as it must and not one moment longer.

— W. E. B. Du Bois, *Darkwater*, 1920

We didn't have any of what they called Civil Rights back then. It was just a matter of survival—existing from day to day.

— Rosa Parks, *Blacks in Detroit*, edited by
Scott & Susan Watson McGehee, 1980

I could see that my significance as an individual was small in this affair. I had become, whether I liked it or not, a symbol representing my people.

— Marian Anderson, from her statement after her
concert at the Lincoln Memorial, April 9, 1939

If we accept and acquiesce in the face of discrimination, we accept the responsibility ourselves and allow those responsible to salve their conscience by believing that they have our acceptance and concurrence. We should, therefore, protest openly everything . . . that smacks of discrimination or slander.

> — Mary McLeod Bethune, "Certain Unalienable Rights," *What the Negro Wants,* edited by Rayford W. Logan, 1944

The Negro himself will more readily acquiesce in his lot unless he has a legally recognized claim to a better life. I think the segregation decision of 1954 probably did more than anything else to awaken the Negro from his apathy to demanding his right to equality.

> — Thurgood Marshall, commenting on the United States Supreme Court's decision in *Brown v. The Board of Education,* 1954

History will have to record that the greatest tragedy of this period of social transition was not the strident clamor of the bad people, but the appalling silence of the good people.

> — Martin Luther King, Jr., *Stride Toward Freedom,* 1958

At the rate things are going here, all of Africa will be free before we can get a lousy cup of coffee.

> — James Baldwin, "A Negro Assays on the
> Negro Mood," *The New York Times*,
> March 12, 1961

The Negro's great stumbling block is not the White Citizen's Counciler or the Ku Klux Klanner, but the white moderate who is more devoted to "order" than to justice . . . who paternalistically believes he can set the timetable for another man's freedom.

> — Martin Luther King, Jr., "Letter from
> Birmingham Jail," April 16, 1963

While I had been fighting in Vietnam alongside brave soldiers trying to preserve their freedom, in my own land a long-simmering conflict had turned into an open fight in our streets and cities—a fight that had to be won.

> — Colin Powell, *The Black 100*, by
> Columbus Salley, 1993

I have a dream that one day on the red hills of Georgia the sons of former slaves and the sons of former slaveowners will be able to sit down together at the table of brotherhood.

— Martin Luther King, Jr., speech at the Civil Rights March on Washington, August 28, 1963

We are not fighting for integration, nor are we fighting for separation. We are fighting for recognition as human beings. We are fighting for . . . human rights.

— Malcolm X, "The Black Revolution," speech, New York, 1964

The day that the black man takes an uncompromising step and realizes that he's within his rights, when his own freedom is being jeopardized, to use any means necessary to bring about his freedom or put a halt to that injustice, I don't think he'll be by himself.

— Malcolm X, Oxford Union Society debate, December 3, 1964

Nonviolence is the answer to the crucial political and moral questions of our time; the need for man to overcome oppression and violence without resorting to oppression and violence. Man must evolve for all human conflict a method which rejects revenge, aggression and retaliation. The foundation of such a method is love.

— Martin Luther King, Jr., speech accepting the Nobel Peace Prize, December 11, 1964

Not one of us will have to raise a sword. Not one gun would we need to fire. The great cannon that will be fired is our unity.

— Elijah Muhammad, *A Message to the Black Man in America*, 1965

Violence is as American as cherry pie.

— H. Rap Brown, press conference, July 27, 1967

You're either part of the solution or part of the problem.

— Eldridge Cleaver, speech, San Francisco, 1968

I had no idea when I refused to give up my seat on that
Montgomery bus that my small action would help put an end
to the segregation laws in the south. I only knew that I was
tired of being pushed around. I was a regular person, just as
good as anybody else. There had been a few times in my life
when I was treated by white people like a regular person, so
I knew what that felt like. It was time. It was time that other
white people started treating me that way.

— Rosa Parks, *Rosa Parks: My Story*, 1992

Sammy Davis, Jr., Duke Ellington, Count Basie, Lena Horne,
Sidney Poitier—we weren't leading the charge. We weren't
at the forefront, getting our heads cracked open, though our
careers were a reflection of what was possible when attention
was paid. Twenty-five years earlier it hadn't been widely
expected, with opportunities so meager, that blacks could be
scientists, statesmen, artists. Every time I stepped out, I felt
the responsibility to do whatever I could to make pending
successes seem a natural expectation.

— Sidney Poitier, *The Measure of A Man:*
A Spiritual Autobiography, 2000

I've been marching since I was seventeen, long before there was a Civil Rights Movement. I was marching through the lobby of the Waldorf-Astoria, of the Sands . . . to a table at the Copa. And I marched alone. Worse. Often to Black derision.

— Sammy Davis, Jr., "Sammy Davis, Jr.:
The Legacy of the World's Greatest Entertainer,"
Ebony, July 1990

What hurt me most about the glorious black awakening of the late sixties and early seventies is that we lost our sense of humor. Many of us thought that enlightened politics excluded it.

— Henry Louis Gates, Jr., *Colored People,* 1994

I am a candidate for the Presidency of the United States. I make that statement proudly, in the full knowledge that, as a black person and as a female person, I do not have a chance of actually gaining that office in this election year.

— Shirley Chisholm, speech, June 4, 1972

It must be remembered that during most of the past 200 years the Constitution as interpreted by this Court did not prohibit the most ingenious and pervasive forms of discrimination against the Negro. Now, when a state acts to remedy the effects of that legacy of discrimination, I cannot believe that this same Constitution stands as a barrier. At every point from birth to death the impact of the past is reflected in the still disfavored position of the Negro. In light of the sorry history of discrimination and its devastating impact on the lives of Negroes, bringing the Negro into the mainstream of American life should be a state interest of the highest order.

— Thurgood Marshall, dissent in *Regents of the University of California v. Bakke*, 1978

My right and my privilege to stand here before you has been won—won in my lifetime—by the blood and the sweat of the innocent.

— Jesse Jackson, speech at Democratic National Convention, Atlanta, Georgia, July 19, 1988

The very class that owes its new affluence to the Movement now refuses to support the organizations that made its success possible, and has retreated from its concern for black people who are poor.

— Alice Walker, "In Search of Our Mothers' Gardens," 1983

A majority of this Court signals that it regards racial discrimination as largely a phenomenon of the past, and that government bodies need no longer preoccupy themselves with rectifying racial injustice . . . I, however, do not believe this nation is anywhere close to eradicating racial discrimination or its vestiges.

— Thurgood Marshall, dissent in *City of Richmond v. Croson*, 1989

I stand before you today as the elected leader of the greatest city of a great nation, to which my ancestors were brought, chained and whipped in the hold of a slave ship. We have not finished the journey toward liberty and justice, but surely we have come a long way.

— David Dinkins, taking the oath of office as mayor of New York City, January 1, 1990

In one generation we have moved from denying a black man service at a lunch counter to elevating one to the highest military office in the nation, and to being a serious contender for the presidency. This is a magnificent country and I am proud to be one of its sons.

> — Colin Powell, announcing his decision not to seek the presidential nomination, Alexandria, Virginia, November 8, 1995

But we believed if we kept on working, if we kept on marching, if we kept on voting, if we kept on believing, we would make America beautiful for everybody.

> — Al Sharpton, speech at Democratic National Convention, 2004

I will never forget that the only reason I'm standing here today is because somebody, somewhere stood up for me when it was risky. Stood up when it was hard. Stood up when it wasn't popular. And because that somebody stood up, a few more stood up. And then a few thousand stood up. And then a few million stood up. And standing up, with courage and clear purpose, they somehow managed to change the world.

> — Barack Obama, speech, Democratic National Committee Fall Meeting, November 30, 2007

America

The life of the nation is secure only while the nation is honest, truthful, and virtuous.

> — Frederick Douglass, speech on the 23rd
> anniversary of Emancipation in the District of
> Columbia, Washington, D.C., April 1885

We are not engaged in domestic politics, in church building or in social uplift work, but we are engaged in nation building.

> — Marcus Garvey, speech, "The Principles of the
> Universal Negro Improvement Association,"
> New York City, November 25, 1922

The destiny of the colored American . . . is the destiny of America.

— Frederick Douglass, speech at the Emancipation
League, Boston, February 12, 1862

If we had been allowed to participate in the vital processes of America's national growth, what would have been the textures of our lives, the pattern of our traditions, the routine of our customs, the state of our arts, the code of our laws, the function of our government! . . . We black folk say that America would have been stronger and greater.

— Richard Wright, *Twelve Million Black Voices*,
1941

We're no more or less than other Americans . . . we're just people . . . white, black, yellow, brown. . . . In our working, our loving, our sorrowing, and our dying we are making America of Now and Tomorrow, just as we helped make it Yesterday.

— Waters E. Turpin, *These Low Grounds*, 1937

My father was a slave and my people died to build this country, and I'm going to stay right here and have a part of it, just like you. And no fascist-minded people like you will drive me from it. Is that clear?

— Paul Robeson, testimony before the House
Un-American Activities Committee,
June 12, 1956

Our children, our jobless men, our deprived, rejected, and starving fellow citizens must come first. For this reason, I intend to vote *No* on every money bill that comes to the floor of this House that provides any funds for the Department of Defense.

— Shirley Chisholm, her first speech to Congress,
March 26, 1969

We have to undo the millions of little white lies that America told itself and the world about the American Black man.

— John O. Killens, "Black Revolution and the
White Backlash," speech given at Town Hall
Forum, New York City, June 15, 1964

The meaning of America is the possibilities of the common man. It is a refutation of that widespread assumption that the real makers of the world must always be a small group of exceptional men, while most men are incapable of assisting civilization or achieving culture. The United States of America proves, if it proves anything, that the number of men who may be educated and may achieve is much larger than the world has hitherto assumed.

> — W. E. B. Du Bois, "What the Negro Has Done for the United States and Texas," address given at the opening of the Hall of Negro Life, 1936

I am particularly struck by the number of aged men who represent America. It seems we are not taking into consideration what is happening in this country today. We are not giving bright young people—who are often so much in touch with the time—a sufficient chance to break into politics and be heard.

> — Shirley Chisholm, quoted in *Shirley Chisholm*, by Susan Brownmiller, 1971

America is me. It gave me the only life I know, so I must share in its survival.

> — Gordon Parks, *Born Black*, 1971

I am America. I am the part you won't recognize. But get used to me. Black, confident, cocky; my name, not yours; my religion, not yours; my goals, my own; get used to me.

> — Muhammad Ali, *The Greatest*, by
> Muhammad Ali with Richard Durham, 1975

Our nation is a rainbow—red, yellow, brown, black, and white—and we're all precious in God's sight.

> — Jesse Jackson, speech given at the Democratic
> National Convention, San Francisco,
> July 17, 1984

At no point in my life have I ever felt as though I were an American.

> — Toni Morrison, *The New York Times*,
> January 5, 1986

I love America more than any other country in the world, and, exactly for this reason, I insist on the right to criticize her perpetually.

> — James Baldwin, *Notes of a Native Son*, 1955

America was the land of education and opportunity. It was a new land to which all people who had youth and a youthful mind turned.

> — Claude McKay, *My Green Hills of Jamaica*, 1946

America is essentially a dream, a dream as yet unfulfilled. It is a dream of a land where men of all races, of all nationalities and of all creeds can live together as brothers.

> — Martin Luther King, Jr., from "The American Dream" speech given at Lincoln University, Oxford, Pennsylvania, June 6, 1961

My heart is filled with love for this country.

> — Barack Obama, *The Audacity of Hope*, 2006

I am not fighting just for myself and my people in the South when I fight for freedom and equality. I realize now that I fight for the moral and political health of America as a whole and for her position in the world at large.

> — Marian Wright Edelman, *The Black 100*, by Columbus Salley, 1993

Hope is what led me here today—with a father from Kenya, a mother from Kansas; and a story that could only happen in the United States of America. Hope is the bedrock of this nation; the belief that our destiny will not be written for us, but by us; by all those men and women who are not content to settle for the world as it is; who have courage to remake the world as it should be.

— Barack Obama, Iowa Caucus Victory speech,
January 3, 2008

For we know that our patchwork heritage is a strength, not a weakness. We are a nation of Christians and Muslims, Jews and Hindus, and non-believers. We are shaped by every language and culture, drawn from every end of this Earth; and because we have tasted the bitter swill of civil war and segregation, and emerged from that dark chapter stronger and more united, we cannot help but believe that the old hatreds shall someday pass; that the lines of tribe shall soon dissolve; that as the world grows smaller, our common humanity shall reveal itself; and that America must play its role in ushering in a new era of peace.

— Barack Obama, the Inaugural Address,
January 21, 2009

Knowledge and Education

Herein lies the tragedy of the age: not that men are poor—all men know something of poverty; not that men are wicked—who is good? Not that men are ignorant—what is truth? Nay, but that men know so little of men.

— W. E. B. Du Bois, *The Souls of Black Folk*, 1903

Nothing in all the world is more dangerous than sincere ignorance and conscientious stupidity.

— Martin Luther King, Jr., *Strength to Love*, 1963

Armed with the knowledge of our past, we can with confidence charter a course for our future.

— Malcolm X, *Malcolm X on Afro-American History*, 1971

Man only truly lives by knowing; otherwise he simply performs, copying the daily habits of others, but conceiving nothing of his creative possibilities as a man, and accepting someone else's superiority and his own misery.

> — Alice Walker, "In Search of Our Mothers' Gardens," 1983

I have always worshipped at the shrine of knowledge knowing that regardless of how much I study, read, travel, expose myself to enriching experiences, I still remain an intellectual pauper.

> — Adam Clayton Powell, Jr., *Adam by Adam*, 1971

I wanted to know the name of every stone and flower and insect and bird and beast. I wanted to know where it got its color, where it got its life—but there was no one to tell me.

> — George Washington Carver, *American Life*, November 1923

My grandfather went to school for one day: to tell the teacher he wouldn't be back. Yet all of his life he read greedily, as did his uneducated friends.

— Toni Morrison, *Black World*, February 1974

It was books that taught me that the things that tormented me most were the very things that connected me with all the people who were alive, or who had ever been alive.

— James Baldwin, *The New York Times*, June 1, 1964

When I read great literature, great drama, speeches, or sermons, I feel that the human mind has not achieved anything greater than the ability to share feelings and thoughts through language.

— James Earl Jones, *Voices and Silences*, 1993

I read to entertain myself, to educate myself, as a way to enlighten myself—as a way to challenge my beliefs about myself.

— LeVar Burton, the *Washington Post*, July 25, 1993

Sometimes folks ask us how we put up with racism and sexism to get our advanced college degrees. How could we stand it? Well, what choice did we have? What choice does anyone have? Life's not easy for anyone, despite how it may look. Sometimes you just have to put up with a lot to get the little bit you need. Now, it's true that you hear of basketball stars and entertainers making it big with no education. But that's only a tiny, tiny number of people. . . . If you are not educated—if you can't write clearly, speak articulately, think logically— you have lost control of your own life.

> — Sarah Delany, *The Delany Sisters' Book of Everyday Wisdom*, by Sarah and A. Elizabeth Delany with Amy Hill Hearth, 1994

I'm not comfortable being preachy, but more people have to start spending as much time in the library as they do on the basketball court. If they took the idea that they could escape poverty through education, I think it would make a more basic and long-lasting change in the way things happen . . . What we need are positive, realistic goals and the willingness to work. Hard work and practical goals.

> — Kareem Abdul-Jabbar, *Kareem*, by Kareem Abdul-Jabbar with Mignon McCarthy, 1990

A mind is a terrible thing to waste.

— United Negro College Fund advertising slogan,
1972

There is no short-cut to improving our schools. The black community itself must take the lead in insisting on quality education. It is self-destructive to get hung up on wanting jive courses, lower standards, and no tests. Our children have to function in a fast-changing society. They have enough cards stacked against them without further handicapping them.

— John E. Jacob, speech, New Orleans,
July 31, 1983

Schooling is what happens inside the walls of the school, some of which is educational. Education happens everywhere, and it happens from the moment a child is born—and some people say before—until a person dies.

— Sara Lawrence-Lightfoot, from *A World of Ideas*,
by Bill Moyers, 1989

Education remains the key to both economic and political empowerment.

> — Barbara Jordan, *Words to Make My Dream Children Live*, edited by Deirdre Mullane, 1995

The answer, for me, begins with what I was most proud of growing up—my education. And I've learned the power of film to educate. With movies you can reach so many people. Without *Glory*, most Americans wouldn't have known about the first infantry of black soldiers that fought for the Union in the Civil War. . . . They wouldn't have known about the bravery of the Fifty-fourth in waging a hellish assault on Fort Wagner in South Carolina, when they were outnumbered and outgunned. I don't know and I can't tell you how many people have approached me and said, I'm so glad they made that movie; I had no idea.

> — Morgan Freeman, "Home," *America Behind the Color Line*, edited by Henry Louis Gates, Jr., 2004

We need a concerted effort in the Black community to reemphasize the importance of education, because knowledge is power. Not power to dominate others, but power to control our own destinies.

> — Johnnie L. Cochran, Jr., "Controlling Our Destinies," *How To Make Black America Better*, edited by Tavis Smiley, 2001

A good education is another name for happiness.

— Ann Plato, *Essays*, 1841

The question is not whether we can afford to invest in every child; it is whether we can afford not to.

— Marian Wright Edelman, *The Measure of Our Success*, 1992

Part of teaching is helping students learn how to tolerate ambiguity, consider possibilities, and ask questions that are unanswerable.

— Sara Lawrence-Lightfoot, *A World of Ideas*, by Bill Moyers, 1989

Love

Love is the most durable power in the world. This creative force is the most potent instrument available in mankind's quest for peace and security.

— Martin Luther King, Jr., *Strength to Love*, 1963

Love has no awareness of merit or demerit; it has no scale by which its portion may be weighed or measured. It does not seek to balance giving and receiving. Love loves; this is its nature.

— Howard Thurman, *Meditations of the Heart*, 1953

Love, I find is like singing. Everybody can do enough to satisfy themselves, though it may not impress the neighbors as being very much.

> — Zora Neale Hurston, *Dust Tracks on a Road*, 1942

The workings of the human heart are the profoundest mystery of the universe. One moment they make us despair of our kind, and the next we see in them the reflection of the divine image.

> — Charles W. Chesnutt, *The Marrow of Tradition*, 1901

To love is to make of one's heart a swinging door.

> — Howard Thurman, *Recapture the Spirit*, 1963

Love stretches your heart and makes you big inside

> — Margaret Walker, *Jubilee*, 1966

We never know we are beings till we love. And then it is we know the powers and the potentialities of human existence, the powers and potentialities of organic, conscious, solar, cosmic matter and force. We, together, vibrate as one in harmony with man and the cosmos.

— Jean Toomer, *The Lives of Jean Toomer*, by
Cynthia Earl Kerman and Richard Eldridge,
1987

Don't threaten me with love, baby. Let's go walking in the rain.

— Billie Holiday, c. 1950

A lost love is like a toothache. It'll hurt you and it'll hurt so much you'll finally get rid of it. You'll miss it but you'll feel better.

— Duke Ellington, *Music Is My Mistress*, 1973

Love does not begin and end the way we seem to think it does. Love is a battle, love is a war; love is growing up.

— James Baldwin, c. 1961

If we love a child, and the child senses that we love him, he will get a concept of love that all subsequent hatred in the world will never be able to destroy.

— Howard Thurman, *Disciplines of Spirit*, 1963

There is always something left to love. And if you ain't learned that, you ain't learning nothing.

— Lorraine Hansberry, *A Raisin in the Sun*, 1959

Marriage, Children, and Family

The heart of marriage is memories; and if the two of you happen to have the same ones and can savor your reruns, then your marriage is a gift from the gods.

— Bill Cosby, *Love and Marriage*, 1989

The long-term accommodation that protects marriage and other such relationships is . . . forgetfulness.

— Alice Walker, *You Can't Keep a Good Woman Down*, 1981

Getting married is easy. Staying married is more difficult. Staying happily married for a lifetime should rank among the fine arts.

— Roberta Flack, widely attributed

One of the realities after years of marriage is that whatever changes you had planned to make for that person are going to happen slowly or not happen at all.

— Bill Cosby, *USA Weekend*, April 7, 1989

I have nothing against intermarriage, except that it means a Negro man is leaving behind the Negro woman who has worked and suffered with him since slavery times.

— Mahalia Jackson, *Movin' on Up*, 1966

For I am my mother's daughter, and the drums of Africa still beat in my heart. They will not let me rest while there is a single Negro boy or girl without a chance to prove his worth.

— Mary McLeod Bethune, "Faith That Moved a Dump Heap," *Who, The Magazine About People*, June 1941

Children's talent to endure stems from their ignorance of alternatives.

— Maya Angelou, *I Know Why the Caged Bird Sings*, 1969

Separate from my boundaries, I had not known before that he had and would have a life beyond being my son, my pretty baby, my cute doll, my charge. In the plowed farmyard near Bakersfield, I began to understand the uniqueness of the person. He was three and I was nineteen, and never again would I think of him as a beautiful appendage of myself.

— Maya Angelou, *Gather Together in My Name*, 1974

Children have never been very good at listening to their elders, but they have never failed to imitate them.

— James Baldwin, *Nobody Knows My Name*, 1961

You know the only people who are *always* sure about the proper way to raise children? Those who've never had any.

— Bill Cosby, *Fatherhood*, 1986

Why do I have to be an example for your kid? *You* be an example for your own kid.

— Bob Gibson, widely attributed

Children make you want to start life over.

— Muhammad Ali, *The Greatest*, by
Muhammad Ali with Richard Durham, 1975

Feeling secure in your worth often stems from knowing you belong to two very special groups—your family and your community.

— Dorothy S. Strickland, *Listen Children*, 1982

A child must have a sense of selfhood, a knowledge that he is not here by sufferance, that his forbears contributed to the country and to the world.

— John O. Killens, *Beyond the Angry Black*, 1966

What children need most is love and attention. That doesn't mean spoiling them or letting them boss you. That doesn't mean letting them do what *they* want to do. But just sit with them, listen to them, look at them. A lot of people don't even *look* at their children. The most important thing is to teach your child compassion. A complete human being is one who can put himself in another's shoes.

— A. Elizabeth Delany, *The Delany Sisters' Book of Everyday Wisdom*, by Sarah and A. Elizabeth Delany with Amy Hill Hearth, 1994

Family is a mixed blessing. You're glad to have one, but it's also like receiving a life sentence for a crime you didn't commit.

— Richard Pryor, *Pryor Convictions*, by Richard Pryor with Todd Gold, 1995

I am not ashamed of my grandparents for having been slaves. I am only ashamed of myself for having at one time been ashamed.

— Ralph Ellison, *Invisible Man*, 1952

My grandmother delivered half a county as midwife and raised other people's kids. She nurtured, and that's something our culture has lost sight of.

— Danny Glover, *Vis à Vis*, October 1991

I do not recollect of ever seeing my mother by the light of day. She would lie down with me and get me to sleep, but long before I waked she was gone.

— Frederick Douglass, *The Life and Times of Frederick Douglass*, 1881

To describe my mother would be to write about a hurricane in its perfect power.

— Maya Angelou, *I Know Why the Caged Bird Sings*, 1969

My mom was the most fantastic woman in the world. She only went to the fifth grade, but she knew there was nothing wrong with my brain, I just couldn't see.

— Ray Charles, *Parade*, October 10, 1988

I had a series of childhood illnesses. It started off as scarlet fever, and from there it was polio. My father was the one who sort of babied me and was sympathetic. He was a determined person. He had to be. There were twenty-two children. I am the twentieth. My mother was the one who made me work, made me believe that one day it would be possible for me to walk without braces.

— Wilma Rudolph, *I Dream a World*, edited by
Barbara Summers and Yvonne Easton, 1999

Even today, when I think about my mother for any reason, what first jumps to mind are memories of her telling me that she loved me more than anyone else in the world.

— Bill Russell, *Second Wind*, 1979

Respectability, achievement, hard work—those were the values my parents lived by, and my mother worked hard to instill them in me.

— Diahann Carroll, *Diahann: An Autobiography*,
by Diahann Carroll with Ross Firestone, 1986

I hope they are still making women like my Momma. She always told me to do the right thing, to have pride in myself and that a good name is better than money.

— Joe Louis, *My Life*, by Joe Louis with
Edna Rust and Art Rust Jr., 1978

My mother never gave up on me. I messed up in school so much they were sending me home, but my mother sent me right back.

— Denzel Washington, *Essence*, November 1986

My mother gave lots of good advice and had a lot to say. And maybe at the time you don't realize it or understand everything, or you don't want to listen, but as you get older, you realize everything she said was true.

— Lenny Kravitz, interview by Dan Neer,
Vivamusic.com

Biology is the least of what makes someone a mother.

— Oprah Winfrey, *Woman's Day*,
October 4, 1988

My mom always taught us that family's all you have when everything's said and done. You have to love them and support them no matter who they are, no matter how they look, no matter how they behave.

— Toni Braxton, *Jet*, May 1994

It was women, then, who provided the ballast in my life— my grandmother, whose dogged practicality kept the family afloat, and my mother, whose love and clarity of spirit kept my sister's and my world centered. Because of them I never wanted for anything important. From them I would absorb the values that guide me to this day.

— Barack Obama, *The Audacity of Hope*, 2006

In African American culture, the least discussed thing amongst men is the fact that they really wish they had fathers. There's a lot of single black women who did the best that they could and that's a beautiful thing, but they don't know how necessary a father is in a kid's life and how much guys miss that deep down inside. That's why they gravitate towards gangs. That's why they gravitate toward older guys who may lead them in a negative direction, because they just want to be embraced by a man.

— LL Cool J, *Sister 2 Sister* magazine, March 2008

I felt something impossible for me to explain in words. Then when they took her away, it hit me. I got scared all over again and began to feel giddy. Then it came to me—I was a father.

— Nat "King" Cole, *Ebony*, March 1950

The truth is that parents are not really interested in justice. They just want quiet.

— Bill Cosby, *Fatherhood*, 1986

My dad has always taught me these words: care and share. That's why we put on clinics. The only thing I can do is try to give back. If it works, it works.

— Tiger Woods, widely attributed

From the first time the doctor placed you in my arms
I knew I'd meet death before I'd let you meet harm.
Although questions arose in my mind, would I be
man enough?

— Will Smith, "Just the Two of Us," 1997

I find myself looking at my children, just watching them and realizing how fortunate I am. Everything I've done on the basketball court, in business, nothing compares to having them.

— Michael Jordan, *Rare Air*, by Michael Jordan, Walter Iooss, and Mark Vancil, 1993

I am the product of hatred and love—the hatred of the social and political structure which dominated the segregated, hate-filled city of my youth, and the love of some people—my mother, my grandparents, my neighbors and relatives—who said by their actions, "You can make it, but first you must endure."

— Clarence Thomas, Commencement speech at Savannah State College, June 9, 1985

When people ask me how did you become who you are, do what you have done, it all goes back to my parents. These were incredible people. They were extraordinary ordinary people. . . . they had this extraordinary belief in the power of education, in the power of opportunity, for me, but not just for me. For the children in the community, and they really tried to see past what Birmingham was in 1960 or '61, the most segregated city, big city in America, a city where you could have had extremely limited horizons. They tried to see past that to what I could be and what other children could be.

— Condoleezza Rice, interview with Charlie Rose, March 18, 2009

Religion

'Twant me, 'twas the Lord. I always told him, "I trust to you. I don't know where to go or what to do, but I expect you to lead me," and he always did.

— Harriet Tubman, to her biographer,
Sarah H. Bradford, c. 1868

I love the pure, peaceable, and impartial Christianity of Christ: I therefore hate the corrupt, slaveholding, women-whipping, cradle-plundering, partial, and hypocritical Christianity of this land.

— Frederick Douglass, *Narrative of the Life of Frederick Douglass*, 1845

Religion without humanity is poor human stuff.

> — Sojourner Truth, speech, Battle Creek,
> Michigan, 1877

Were I to be again reduced to the chains of slavery, next to that enslavement, I should regard being the slave of a religious master the greatest calamity that could befall me . . . they are the worst, the basest, the meanest, the most cruel and cowardly of all others.

> — Frederick Douglass, *Life and Times of
> Frederick Douglass*, 1881

Any religion that professes to be concerned with the souls of men and is not concerned with the slums that damn them, and the social conditions that cripple them, is a dry-as-dust religion.

> — Martin Luther King, Jr., *Stride Toward Freedom*,
> 1958

I conceive of God, in fact, as a means of liberation and not a means to control others.

> — James Baldwin, from "In Search of a Majority,"
> address given at Kalamazoo College,
> February 1960

My religion has come to mean more to me than ever before. I have come to believe more and more in a personal God— not a process, but a person, a creative power with infinite love who answers prayers.

> — Martin Luther King, Jr., *Redbook*,
> September 1961

I feel a real *kinship* with God, and that's what has helped me pull out of the problems I've faced. Anybody who has kept up with my career knows that I've had my share of problems and trouble, but look at me today . . . Through the years, no matter how much success I achieved, I never lost my faith in God.

> — Aretha Franklin, *Essence*, 1971

My hope for my children must be that they respond to the still, small voice of God in their own hearts.

— Andrew Young, *A Way Out of No Way*, 1994

Have faith in God. Do not be tempted either by pleasures and material possessions, or by the claims of science and smart thinkers, into believing that religion is obsolete, that the worship of God is somehow beneath you. Spiritual nourishment is as important as physical nourishment, or intellectual nourishment. The religion you choose is not nearly as important as a fundamental faith in God.

— Arthur Ashe, from a letter to his daughter in *Days of Grace*, by Arthur Ashe and Arnold Rampersad, 1993

My mother gave me something to live on if she weren't around—spirituality and faith. She gave me her base, her spiritual base, her unshakeable base.

— Gladys Knight, *Ebony*, May 1992

I remember when I got married, I stopped reading the Bible. When my mother found out that I had stopped, she told me that one should not stop reading the Bible; there was always something new to learn by reading it. On that day, I started back reading the Bible and have not stopped since.

— Rosa Parks, quoted in *My Mother Had a Dream*, edited by Tamara Nikuradse, 1996

Don't pray when it rains if you don't pray when the sun shines.

— Satchel Paige, c. 1945

Trouble follows a sin as sure as a fever follows a chill.

— Anonymous

To be a Christian is to have a joyful attitude toward the resurrection claim, to stake one's life on it, and to rest one's hope upon its promise—the promise of a new heaven and new earth.

— Cornel West, *Prophetic Fragments*, 1988

When you meet an American Negro who's not a Methodist or a Baptist, some white man's been tampering with his religion.

— Booker T. Washington, *Selected Speeches of Booker T. Washington*, 1932

I am a Muslim and . . . my religion makes me be against all forms of racism. It keeps me from judging any man by the color of his skin. It teaches me to judge him by his deeds and his conscious behavior. And it teaches me to be for the rights of all human beings, but especially the Afro-American human being, because my religion is a natural religion, and the first law of nature is self-preservation.

— Malcolm X, speech, New York, 1965

If we can put the names of our faiths aside for the moment and look at principles, we will find a common thread running through all the great religious expressions.

— Louis Farrakhan, c. 1993

Over the years my religion has changed and my spirituality
has evolved. Religion and spirituality are very different,
but people often confuse the two. Some things cannot be
taught, but they can be awakened in the heart. Spirituality
is recognizing the divine light that is within us all. It doesn't
belong to any particular religion; it belongs to everyone.

— Muhammad Ali, *The Soul of a Butterfly*, by
Muhammad Ali with Hana Yasmeen Ali, 2004

Work and Artistry

The return from your work must be the satisfaction which that work brings you and the world's need of that work. With this, life is heaven, or as near heaven as you can get. Without this—with work which you despise, which bores you, and which the world does not need—this life is hell.

> — W. E. B. Du Bois, address on his 90th birthday
> to his newly born great-grandson, 1958

Art must discover and reveal the beauty which prejudice and caricature have overlaid.

> — Alain Locke, "The Legacy of the Ancestral Arts,"
> 1925

All art is a kind of confession, more or less oblique. All artists, if they are to survive, are forced, at last, to tell the whole story, to vomit the anguish up.

— James Baldwin, *Nobody Knows My Name:*
More Notes of a Native Son, 1961

The same music governs the rhythm of the seasons, the pulse of our heartbeats, the migration of the birds, the ebb and flow of ocean tides, the cycles of growth, evolution and dissolution. It's music, it's rhythm.

— Michael Jackson, *Michael Jackson*
by Catherine Dineen, 1993

This is one of the glories of man, the inventiveness of the human mind and the human spirit: Whenever life doesn't seem to give us vision, we create one.

— Lorraine Hansberry, quoted in *The African*
American Century, by Henry Louis Gates, Jr.,
and Cornel West, 2000

Through their untarnishable beauty, they seem assured of the immortality of those great folk expressions that survive not so much through being typical of a group or representative of a period as by virtue of being fundamentally and everlastingly human.

— Alain Locke, "The Negro Spirituals," 1925

The songs of the slaves represent the sorrows of his heart; and he is relieved by them, only as an aching heart is relieved by its tears.

— Frederick Douglass, *Narrative of the Life of Frederick Douglass*, 1845

The function of the music is to raise both performer and audience far above routine emotion; the elderly throw away their sticks and dance.

—John Lovell Jr., *Black Song*, 1972

Gospel music in those days of the early 1930s was really taking wing. It was the kind of music colored people had left behind them down south and they liked it because it was just like a letter from home.

— Mahalia Jackson, c. 1966

The memory of things gone is important to a jazz musician. Things like old folks singing in the moonlight in the back yard on a hot night or something said long ago.

— Louis Armstrong, *The New Yorker*, July 8, 1944

It makes no diff'rence if it's sweet or hot
Just give that rhythm ev'rything you got
It don't mean a thing, if it ain't got that swing

— "It Don't Mean a Thing (If It Ain't Got That Swing)," music by Duke Ellington, lyrics by Irving Mills, 1932

Man, if you gotta ask you'll never know.

— Louis Armstrong, his reply when asked what jazz is

I wouldn't sing to segregated audiences, so I sang in Negro schools and white people came.

> — Paul Robeson, *People's Voice*, May 22, 1945

The Cotton Club—smack dab in the middle of Harlem—but Black people couldn't go there. It was for whites only. The club featured Black entertainment and some of the most gorgeous Black women that could be found.

> — Joe Louis, *My Life*, by Joe Lewis with Edna and Art Rust Jr., 1978

The price one pays for pursuing any profession or calling is an intimate knowledge of its ugly side.

> — James Baldwin, *Nobody Knows My Name: More Notes of a Native Son*, 1961

I just came here to entertain you. That was what I thought you wanted. I was born here.

> — Nat "King" Cole, after being beaten up on stage by group of white supremacists, Birmingham, Alabama, April 10, 1956, quoted in *The African American Century*, edited by Henry Louis Gates, Jr., and Cornel West, 2000

The day I no longer go on stage will be the day I die.

> — Josephine Baker, quoted in *The African American Century*, by Henry Louis Gates, Jr., and Cornel West, 2000

My mother wanted me to be a star and I worked hard for her goal.

> — Lena Horne, *Lena*, by Lena Horne and Richard Schickel, 1965

It's not the public that inspires an artist to create. An artist feels the need to create even if there is no public. If there were no one on the planet I'd still do funny things. I'd just be laughing by myself.

> — Eddie Murphy, *Playboy*, February 1990

Music is your own experience, your thoughts, your wisdom. If you don't live it, it won't come out of your horn. They teach you there's a boundary line to music. But, man, there's no boundary line to art.

> — Charlie Parker, *Hear Me Talkin' to Ya*, by Nat Shapiro and Nat Hentoff, 1955

While waiting for my mother to finish cooking dinner . . . in fifteen minutes I wrote the score "Mood Indigo." "Black and Tan Fantasy" was written in a taxicab on the way to a recording session. In each case it was a matter of deadlines. Standing up against the studio's glass enclosure I wrote the score for "Solitude" in twenty minutes.

— Duke Ellington, *Music Is My Mistress*, 1973

I can't express myself in easy conversation—the words just don't come out right. But when I get up on stage—well, that's my whole life. *That's* my religion.

— Jimi Hendrix, interview, London, 1969

When I'm on stage, I'm trying to do one thing: bring people joy. Just like church does. People don't go to church to find trouble, they go there to lose it.

— James Brown, *The Godfather of Soul*,
by James Brown with Bruce Tucker, 1986

Nothing can harm me when I'm on stage—nothing. That's really me. That's what I'm here to do. I'm totally at home on stage. That's where I live. That's where I was born. That's where I'm safe.

— Michael Jackson, *Michael Jackson*
by Catherine Dineen, 1993

Black music has always been the prologue to social change.

— Quincy Jones, *Playboy*, July 1990

Got to give us what we want
Gotta give us what we need
Our freedom of speech is freedom or death
We got to fight the powers that be

— Public Enemy, "Fight the Power," 1989

People need to stop sleeping. . . . Hip-hop is not a music that you sit down and listen to and that's it. It gives you a lot of answers . . . but it also gives you a lot of questions.

— Queen Latifah, *Christian Science Monitor*,
November 4, 1991

It's a difficult path to get here, and I don't, by no means, want to advocate not getting your education, but for us, for me specifically, education for me was to articulate what was on my mind, right? Because I had a gift to make music . . . and a gift not only just to make songs but to share my experiences and things that I went through and the intelligence to get to the details of it.

> — Jay-Z, interview together with Mary J. Blige
> on *The Tavis Smiley Show*, April 2008

I was attracted to the sound and the content and the freedom of rap. To me, it's like a free art form. It flows—it's smooth. It can be anything you want it to be—harsh, bitter, funny, you name it.

> — Queen Latifah, *Los Angeles Times*,
> September 8, 1991

My life has largely been about promoting the anger, style, aggression, and attitude of urban America to a worldwide audience. I've created a business that didn't exist a generation ago.

> — Russell Simmons, *Life and Def: Sex, Drugs,*
> *Money & God*, 2002

Not all rap music is about whores and bitches. . . . Much of
rap is about the conditions under which rappers live. It's
a language they have developed to describe what they go
through. They're putting it on record for everyone to hear.

— Berry Gordy, *Playboy*, August 1995

I knew Snoop Dog didn't start misogyny. I knew that Tupac
Shakur didn't start sexism and God knows that Dr. Dre didn't
start patriarchy. Yet they extended it in vicious form within
their own communities. They made vulnerable people more
vulnerable. But at the same time, we know that traditions of
misogyny and sexism and patriarchy are deep and profound
and as American as apple pie.

— Michael Eric Dyson, speech,
Washington, D.C., 2005

I think that if we continue to separate ourselves as black
or white artists then we separate ourselves from a larger
audience. I just happen to be black, which I feel is an attribute,
but it shouldn't be an issue. Art has to be more universal.

— Mildred Howard, *Connecting Conversations*,
1988

All token blacks have the same experience. I have been
pointed at as a solution to things that have not begun to
be solved, because pointing at us token blacks eases the
conscience of millions, and I think this is dreadfully wrong.

— Leontyne Price, c. 1959

I don't want to be put on a pedestal. I just want to be
reasonably successful and live a normal life with all the
conveniences to make it so. I think I've already got the main
thing I've always wanted, which is to be somebody, to have
identity. I'm Althea Gibson, the tennis champion. I hope it
makes me happy.

— Althea Gibson, *I Always Wanted
to Be Somebody*, 1958

After I came home from the 1936 Olympics with my four
medals, it became increasingly apparent that everyone was
going to slap me on the back, want to shake my hand, or have
me up to their suite. But no one was going to offer me a job.

— Jesse Owens, *The Black 100*,
by Columbus Salley, 1993

At the beginning of the World Series of 1947, I experienced a completely new emotion when the National Anthem was played. This time, I thought, it is being played for me, as much as for anyone else. This is organized major league baseball, and I am standing here with all the others, and everything that takes place includes me.

— Jackie Robinson, *This I Believe*, series hosted by
Edward R. Murrow, January 1951

Life is a gamble. You can get hurt, but people die in plane crashes, lose their arms and legs in car accidents; people die every day. Same with fighters: some die, some get hurt, some go on. You just don't let yourself believe it will happen to you.

— Muhammad Ali, *I Am King:
Photographic Biography of Muhammad Ali*,
by David King, 1975

Once I get the ball you're at my mercy. There is nothing you can say or do about it. I own the ball . . . When I'm on my game I don't think there's anybody that can stop me.

— Michael Jordan, *GQ*, March 1989

Poverty and Riches

Money is the root of every mess you can think of. There's some folks who would kill you for a nickel. Those are the sorriest folks of all. Anyone who lives for money is surely missing the best things in life. There's satisfaction in doing, in helping. There's an old saying, "Money is useful, but don't let it use you."

— A. Elizabeth Delany, *The Delany Sisters' Book of Everyday Wisdom*, by Sarah and A. Elizabeth Delany with Amy Hill Hearth, 1994

A race which cannot save its earnings can never rise in the scale of civilization.

— Frederick Douglass, *North American Review*, 1884

And when you're poor, you grow up fast.

— Billie Holiday, *Lady Sings the Blues*,
by Billie Holiday with William Duffy, 1956

The rich rob the poor and the poor rob one another.

— Sojourner Truth, attributed

We were Poor. I'm spelling it with a capital P . . . we were on the bottom of the ladder looking up at everyone else. Nothing below us 'cept the ground.

— Ray Charles, *Brother Ray*, by Ray Charles
with David Ritz, 1978

Anyone who has ever struggled with poverty knows how extremely expensive it is to be poor; and if one is a member of a captive population, economically speaking, one's feet have simply been placed on the treadmill forever. One is victimized, economically speaking, in a thousand ways.

— James Baldwin, *Nobody Knows My Name:
More Notes of a Native Son*, 1961

Material deprivation is horrible, but it does not compare to spiritual deprivation.

— Ossie Davis, *City Arts Quarterly*, Spring 1988

It's easy to be independent when you've got money. But to be independent when you haven't got a thing—that's the Lord's test.

— Mahalia Jackson, c. 1966

The greatest thing I ever was able to do was give a welfare check back.

— Whoopi Goldberg, *Ebony*, March 1991

Affluence separates people. Poverty knits 'em together. You got some sugar and I don't; I borrow some of yours. Next month you might not have any flour; well, I'll give you some of mine.

— Ray Charles, *Brother Ray*, by Ray Charles with David Ritz, 1978

When you ain't got no money, you gotta get an attitude.

— Richard Pryor, *Richard Pryor: Black and Blue,*
by Jeff Rovin, 1983

Everybody in the ghetto aspires to get out. Nobody with sense
wants to live there with rats, roaches, crime and drugs.

— Ice-T, *Los Angeles Times,* March 21, 1993

All the money in the world will not buy you a kid who will do
homework, or maturity for a kid who needs it. It may buy a
kid who knows how to buy.

— Bill Cosby, 1985

I used to think something was wrong with me because I never
understood that I was poor. I never understood that I was
having to struggle, because the way I thought, I really wasn't.
I thought I had it all. I was so much at peace and I was so much
into the total surroundings of my family, my grandparents, my
mother, and the true love, the true essence of the word "love."
I didn't know what all that other stuff was until they passed.

— Bernie Mac, "The Chameleon," *America Behind
the Color Line,* edited by Henry Louis Gates, Jr.,
2004

Money, it turned out, was exactly like sex. You thought of nothing else if you didn't have it and thought of other things if you did.

— James Baldwin, "The Black Boy Looks at the
White Boy," *Esquire*, May 1961

I don't like money actually, but it quiets my nerves.

— Joe Louis, c. 1965

Growing up, I never had much money, although we were not poor. My father taught me to be prudent and temperate with money. Use money; do not let money use you. Spend wisely. Your income and wealth should provide for these basics: a comfortable home, the best education that you can afford, health insurance for your family, charitable donations to those in need, and a sum of money saved and never touched except for emergencies. However much you have or make, beware of living beyond your means.

— Arthur Ashe, from a letter to his daughter
in *Days of Grace*, by Arthur Ashe and Arnold
Rampersad, 1993

All the money in the world doesn't mean a thing if you don't have time to enjoy it.

> — Oprah Winfrey, *Ladies' Home Journal*,
> December 1988

Poverty is not about color.

> — Queen Latifah, *Detroit Free Press*,
> March 8, 1992

Women

To be Black and be a woman. To be a double outsider, to be twice oppressed, to be more than invisible.

— Julius Lester, introduction to *Some Changes*, by June Jordan, 1971

That man . . . says that women need to be helped into carriages, and lifted over ditches, and to have the best place everywhere. Nobody ever helps me into carriages, or over mud puddles, or gives me any best place, and ain't I a woman? . . . I have plowed, and planted, and gathered into barns, and no man could head me—and ain't I a woman? I could work as much and eat as much as a man (when I could get it), and bear the lash as well—and ain't I a woman? I have borne thirteen children and seen them most all sold off into slavery, and when I cried out with a mother's grief, none but Jesus heard—and ain't I a woman?

— Sojourner Truth, speech at Women's Rights Convention, Akron, Ohio, 1851

True chivalry respects all womanhood. . . . Virtue knows no color lines, and the chivalry which depends upon complexion of skin and texture of hair can command no honest respect.

— Ida B. Wells, *A Red Record*, 1895

That . . . man . . . says women can't have as much rights as man, cause Christ wasn't a woman. Where did your Christ come from? . . . From God and a woman. Man had nothing to do with him.

— Sojourner Truth, speech at Women's Rights Convention, Akron, Ohio, 1851

The difference between white and black females seemed to me an eminently satisfactory one. White females were *ladies*, said the sign maker, worthy of respect. And the quality that made ladyhood worthy? Softness, helplessness and modesty— which I interpreted as a willingness to let others do their labor and their thinking. Colored females, on the other hand, were *women*—unworthy of respect, independent and immodest.

— Toni Morrison, "What the Black Woman Thinks About Women's Lib," *The New York Times Magazine*, August 22, 1971

I'm a woman. I'm a black woman. I'm a poor woman. I'm a fat woman. I'm a middle-aged woman. And I'm on welfare. In this country if you're any one of those things, you count less as a person. If you're all those things, you just don't count, except as a statistic. I am a statistic.

— Johnnie Tillmon, "Welfare is a
Woman's Issue," 1972

Every Black woman in America lives her life somewhere along a wide curve of ancient and unexpressed anger.

— Audre Lorde, *Sister Outsider*, 1974

I don't know everything, I just do everything.

— Toni Morrison, *Sula*, 1974

My grandmother, who was one of the greatest human beings I've ever known, used to say, "I am a child of God and I'm nobody's creature." That to me defined the Black woman through the centuries.

— Maya Angelou, *Essence*, December 1992

Black womanhood is outraged and humiliated. Black womanhood cries for dignity and restitution and salvation. Black womanhood wants and needs protection, and keeping and holding. Who will assuage her indignation? Who will keep her precious and pure? Who will glorify and proclaim her beautiful image? To whom will she cry rape?

— Abbey Lincoln, "Who Will Revere the Black Woman?," *Negro Digest*, September 1966

But I think women dwell quite a bit on the duress under which they work, on how hard it is just to do it at all. We are traditionally rather proud of ourselves for having slipped creative work in there between the domestic chores and obligations. I'm not sure we deserve such big A-pluses for all that.

— Toni Morrison, *Newsweek*, March 30, 1981

Guided by my heritage of a love of beauty and a respect for strength—in search of my mother's garden, I found my own.

— Alice Walker, "In Search of Our Mothers' Gardens," 1983

The best judge of whether or not a country is going to develop is how it treats its women. If it's educating its girls, if women have equal rights, that country is going to move forward. But if women are oppressed and abused and illiterate, then they're going to fall behind.

— Barack Obama, *Ladies' Home Journal*,
September 2008

Speaking to Young People

Always know that there is unlimited power in a developed mind and a disciplined spirit. If your mind can conceive it and your heart can believe it, you can achieve it. Suffering breeds character; character breeds faith, and in the end, faith will prevail. Armed with this knowledge and a faith in God, you can turn minuses into pluses; you can turn stumbling blocks into stepping stones.

— Jesse Jackson, c. 1993

Do not let yourself be overwhelmed! If you are wise, strong enough to survive the threatening atmosphere of the streets, then channel that same energy into thriving in that same atmosphere at your school.

— Bill Cosby, *Ebony*, June 1993

I want you to find strength in your diversity. Let the fact that you are black or yellow or white be a source of pride and inspiration to you. Draw strength from it. Let it be someone else's problem, but never yours. Never hide behind it or use it as an excuse for not doing your best.

— Colin Powell, Commencement address,
Fisk University, May 4, 1992

After you graduate today, even if you have no job, you can work at treating human beings with the values they have, made by God.

— Bill Cosby, Commencement address,
University of Maryland, May 19, 1992

Whether or not you reach your goals in life depends entirely on how well you prepare for them and how badly you want them. . . . You're eagles! Stretch your wings and fly to the sky!

— Ronald McNair, widely attributed

Deal with yourself as an individual worthy of respect, and make everyone else deal with you the same way.

— Nikki Giovanni, *Proud Sisters*, edited by
Diane J. Johnson, 1995

I've hit 755 home runs, and I did it without putting a needle in my arm or a whiskey bottle in my mouth.

— Hank Aaron, speech at dedication of baseball
field, Mobile, Alabama, 1991

There ain't no joy in a high—none. You *think* there's a joy in a high because it feels good temporarily. But it feels good less and less often, so you've got to do it more and more often. It ain't your friend.

— Whoopi Goldberg, *Ebony*, March 1991

No matter how good they say you are, always keep working on your game.

— Michael Jordan, advice to Tiger Woods,
as reported in *Time*

It isn't where you came from; it's where you're going that counts.

— Ella Fitzgerald, *Ella Fitzgerald,*
by Stuart Nicholson, 1994

Trust yourself. Think for yourself. Act for yourself. Speak for yourself. Be yourself. Imitation is suicide.

— Marva Collins, c. 1988

Don't have babies before you're ready—and "ready" means being married! Raising children is the hardest work you'll ever do. It's selfish to deny a child its best chances in life, and it's foolish to deny yourself a future.

— Sarah and A. Elizabeth Delany, *The Delany Sisters' Book of Everyday Wisdom,* by Sarah and A. Elizabeth Delany with Amy Hill Hearth, 1994

Focusing your life solely on making a buck shows a poverty of ambition. It asks too little of yourself. You need to take up the challenges that we face as a nation and make them your own. Not because you have a debt to all of those who helped you get where you are, although you do have that debt. Not because you have an obligation to those who are less fortunate, although you do have that obligation. You need to take on the challenge because you have an obligation to yourself. Because our individual salvation depends on collective salvation. Because it's only when you hitch your wagon to something larger than yourself that you will realize your true potential. And if we're willing to share the risks and the rewards this new century offers, it will be a victory for each of you, and for every American.

— Barack Obama, Commencement address,
Knox College, June 4, 2005

Yesterday, Today, and Tomorrow

Let the Afro-American depend on no party, but on himself for his salvation. Let him continue to education, character, and above all, put money in his purse.

— Ida B. Wells, "Iola's Southern Field,"
The New York Age, November 11, 1892

If the house is to be set in order, one cannot begin with the present; he must begin with the past.

— John Hope Franklin, *The Black 100*,
by Columbus Salley, 1993

There is a way to look at the past. Don't hide from it. It will not catch you if you don't repeat it.

— Pearl Bailey, *Black Pearls*,
by Eric V. Copage, 1993

The only time we should look back to yesterday is to look at the positive things that were accomplished to encourage us to do better things today and tomorrow.

— Stevie Wonder, *Rolling Stone*,
November 5, 1987

Everything took a lot longer way back when, but you know what? People weren't as frantically busy. Being busy is fine, it's healthy, it's exciting, but folks today just seem to zoom through life! In our day, people had to work hard, so they were tired. They were tired, but they weren't as crazed as folks today.

— Sarah Delany, *The Delany Sisters' Book of
Everyday Wisdom*, by Sarah and A. Elizabeth
Delany with Amy Hill Hearth, 1994

Personal success can be no answer. It can no longer be a question of an Anderson, a Robinson, a Jackson, or a Robeson. It must be the question of the well-being and opportunities not of a few but for all of the great Negro people of which I am a part.

— Paul Robeson, *Milwaukee Journal*,
October 20, 1941

Black people are destroying themselves, their sense of humanity is being twisted into a philosophy of dog-eat-dog, get what you can and exploit each other if you have to.

— Amy Garvey, "Mrs. Garvey Talks
with Ida Lewis," *Encore*, May 1973

I don't believe in planning for the future. I believe in planning for now.

— Ray Charles, *Brother Ray*, by Ray Charles
with David Ritz, 1978

I live a day at a time. Each day I look for a kernel of excitement. In the morning, I say: "What is my exciting thing for today?" Then, I do the day. Don't ask me about tomorrow.

— Barbara C. Jordan, *Parade*, February 16, 1986

Nothing the future brings can defeat a people who have come through three hundred years of slavery and humiliation and privation with heads high and eyes clear and straight.

— Paul Robeson, speech, New Orleans,
October 29, 1942

Whatever future America will have will be directly related to the solving of its racial dilemma, which is a human dilemma.

— John A. Williams, *Beyond the Angry Black*,
1966

I am overwhelmed by the grace and persistence of my people.

— Maya Angelou, *Essence*, December 1992

To continue to repeat the same old stale formulas—to blame, in exactly the same way, "the man" for oppressing us all, to scapegoat Koreans, Jews, or even Haitians for seizing local entrepreneurial opportunities that have, for whatever reason, eluded us—is to fail to accept moral leadership. Not to demand that each member of the Black community accept individual responsibility for their behavior—whether that behavior assumes the form of gang violence, unprotected sexual activity, you name it—is another way of selling out a beleaguered community.

> — Henry Louis Gates, Jr., "Hard Truths,"
> *How to Make Black America Better*,
> edited by Tavis Smiley, 2001

When I look at the future it's so bright it burns my eyes.

> — Oprah Winfrey, *Reader's Digest*, February 1988

Words of Wisdom

I don't let my mouth say nothing my head can't stand.

— Louis Armstrong, *Life*, April 15, 1956

Avoid fried meats which angry up the blood. If your stomach disputes you, lie down and pacify it with cool thoughts. Keep the juices flowing by jangling around gently as you move. Go very light on the vices, such as carrying on in society. The social ramble ain't restful. Avoid running at all times. Don't look back. Something might be gaining on you.

— Satchel Paige, *How to Stay Young*,
originally published in *Collier's*, 1953

If I'd known I was going to live this long, I'd have taken better care of myself.

— Eubie Blake, widely attributed

The battles that count aren't the ones for gold medals. The struggles within yourself—the invisible, inevitable battles inside all of us—that's where it's at.

— Jesse Owens, *Blackthink*, 1970

Fear of something is at the root of hate for others, and hate within will eventually destroy the hater. Keep your thoughts free from hate, and you need have no fear from those who hate you.

— George Washington Carver, quoted in
George Washington Carver: Scientist and Symbol, by Linda O. McMurray, 1982

Start from the bottom up and work like a son of a gun.

— Fats Waller, c. 1950

I can accept failure. Everyone fails at something. But I can't accept not trying.

— Michael Jordan, *I Can't Accept Not Trying*,
by Michael Jordan and Mark Vancil, 1994

Success is to be measured not so much by the position that one has reached in life as by the obstacles which he has overcome while trying to succeed.

— Booker T. Washington, *Up from Slavery*, 1901

Take advantage of every opportunity; where there is none, make it for yourself, and let history record that as we toiled laboriously and courageously, we worked to live gloriously.

— Marcus Garvey, *Garvey and Garveyism*,
by Amy Jacques Garvey, 1963

Anytime you see someone more successful than you are, they are doing something that you aren't.

— Malcolm X, *The Autobiography of Malcolm X*, 1965

Opportunities are there, but we can't start out as vice-president. Even if we landed such a position, it wouldn't do us any good because we wouldn't know how to do our work. It's better to start where we fit in, then work our way up.

> — Benjamin Carson, *Gifted Hands*,
> by Benjamin Carson with Cecil Murphey, 1990

If you run into a wall, don't turn around and give up. Figure out how to climb it, go through it, or work around it.

> — Michael Jordan, *I Can't Accept Not Trying*,
> by Michael Jordan and Mark Vancil, 1994

I never thought of losing, but now that it's happened, the only thing is to do it right. That's my obligation to all the people who believe in me. We all have to take defeats in life.

> — Muhammad Ali, statement after losing
> his fight to Ken Norton, 1973

If you're going to play the game properly you'd better know every rule.

> — Barbara C. Jordan, *Ebony*, February 1975

Success is the result of perfection, hard work, learning from failure, loyalty, and persistence.

— Colin Powell, *Ebony*, July 1988

I will not listen myself, and I will not have you listen to the nonsense that no people can succeed in life among people by whom they have been despised and oppressed.

— Frederick Douglass, *Life and Times of Frederick Douglass*, 1881

Blacks ought to help themselves more and stop crying about what they don't get. It's true they don't get that much, but stop crying about it and go on and get more.

— John Hope Franklin, *Emerge*, March 1994

Freedom from alien substances like drugs. Life is a secret lease from God and we should not allow ourselves to be bruised. Family life is our strength and success.

— Joseph Lowery, *USA Today*, March 8, 1985

Just remember one thing: Manners and behavior can take you where money can't take you, regardless of what color you are in America.

— Bill "Bojangles" Robinson, attributed

Make your success work to help others achieve their measures of success and hope they, in turn, will do likewise. This is the kind of chain reaction that is music to my ears.

— Berry Gordy, c. 1989

Black men who have succeeded have an obligation to serve as role models for young men entrapped by a vicious cycle of poverty, despair, and hopelessness.

— Benjamin Hooks, "Publisher's Foreword," in *Crisis*, March 1986

Once you have experienced a failure or a disappointment, once you've analyzed it and gotten the lessons out of it— dump it.

— Colin Powell, *Parade*, August 13, 1989

I thought I could change the world. It took me a hundred years to figure out I can't change the world. I can only change Bessie. And honey, that ain't easy either.

— A. Elizabeth Delany, *Having Our Say*,
by Sarah and A. Elizabeth Delany with
Amy Hill Hearth, 1993

Believe in life! Always human beings will live and progress to greater, broader, and fuller life.

— W. E. B. Du Bois, *Last Message
to the World*, 1957

About the Contributors

HANK AARON (B. 1934) — Baseball player, famous for breaking Babe Ruth's home run record in 1974 (retired with 755 home runs), won one World Series with the Milwaukee Braves, National Baseball Hall of Fame Inductee.

KAREEM ABDUL-JABBAR (B. 1947) — Basketball player, coach, broadcaster, writer. Led the Los Angeles Lakers to five NBA Championships, Basketball Hall of Fame inductee.

ALVIN AILEY (1931–1989) — Dancer, choreographer, founder of the Alvin Ailey American Dance Theater in New York.

MUHAMMAD ALI (B. 1942) — Boxer, humanitarian, activist, three-time winner of World Heavyweight Championship, winner of Olympic Gold medal in 1960, recipient of countless awards and honors including of Spirit of America Award and Presidential Medal of Freedom. Travels the world for humanitarian causes.

MARIAN ANDERSON (1897–1993) — Opera singer and leading contralto of her day. She gave legendary concert in front of Lincoln Memorial after being barred from performing at Constitution Hall in Washington D.C. Recipient of Presidential Medal of Freedom and Congressional Gold Medal, National Medal of Arts, Grammy Lifetime Achievement Award, and Kennedy Center honoree.

MAYA ANGELOU (B. 1928) — Writer of poetry, prose, and autobiographical works, actress, activist, educator, composer, winner of scores of honors and awards including Grammys, Presidential Medal of Arts, and Lincoln Medal. Her first autobiographical work *I Know Why the Caged Bird Sings* (1969) brought her international acclaim.

LOUIS ARMSTRONG (1901–1971) — Cornet and trumpet player, singer, improviser, leading influence in jazz. Winner of Grammy Lifetime Achievement Award, Grammy Hall of Fame inductee, Rock and Roll Hall of Fame inductee, Big Band and Jazz Hall of Fame inductee, Jazz Hall of Fame at Lincoln Center inductee, Down Beat and Jazz Hall of Fame inductee.

ARTHUR ASHE (1943–1993) — Tennis player, winner of three Grand Slam titles, Presidential Medal of Freedom recipient, Tennis Hall of Fame inductee.

JOSEPHINE BAKER (1906–1975) — Dancer, singer, actress, French Resistance operative.

JAMES BALDWIN (1924–1987) — Writer of plays, novels, and essays; civil rights activist.

CHARLES BARKLEY (B. 1963) — Basketball player, U.S. Gold Medal Olympiad, Basketball Hall of Fame inductee, television commentator.

HALLE BERRY (B. 1966) — Actress, first African American to win Academy Award for Best Actress, Golden Globe Winner, Emmy Award winner.

MARY MCLEOD BETHUNE (1875–1955) — Educator, activist, special advisor to Presidents Franklin Delano Roosevelt and Harry Truman.

EUBIE BLAKE (1883–1983) — Pianist, composer, lyricist, wrote string of Broadway hits, recipient of Presidential Medal of Freedom, inductee in Big Band and Jazz Halls of Fame.

TONI BRAXTON (B. 1967) — Singer, songwriter, actress, winner of multiple Grammy Awards.

CLAUDE BROWN (1937–2002) — Lawyer, writer.

H. RAP BROWN (B. 1943) — Political activist. In 1972 he went to prison for armed robbery. In prison, he converted to Islam and changed his name to Jamil Abdullah Al-Amin. He currently leads a mosque in Atlanta.

JAMES BROWN (1933–2006) — Singer, songwriter, dancer, producer, Grammy Award winner, Grammy Lifetime Achievement Award winner, Songwriters Hall of Fame inductee, Kennedy Center honoree.

LEVAR BURTON (B. 1957) — Actor, director, writer, activist. Winner of Grammy Award and several Daytime Emmy Awards as performer and executive producer for PBS series *Reading Rainbow*.

DIAHANN CARROLL (B. 1935) — Actress, Tony Award winner, Golden Globe Winner.

BENJAMIN CARSON (B. 1951) — Neurosurgeon, writer, Presidential Medal of Freedom recipient.

GEORGE WASHINGTON CARVER (1864–1943) — Scientist, botanist, educator, inventor. Best known for his work developing products from peanuts.

RAY CHARLES (1930–2004) — Blind singer-songwriter, musician, arranger, bandleader, actor, Rock and Roll Hall of Fame inductee, Grammy Award winner, Grammy Lifetime Achievement Award winner, Kennedy Center honoree.

CHARLES W. CHESNUTT (1858–1932) — Writer, educator, political activist.

SHIRLEY CHISHOLM (B. 1924) — Educator, politician, writer. First African American woman to be elected to Congress (1968–1982). In 1972, she made a bid for the Democratic presidential nomination, again making history. National Women's Hall of Fame inductee.

ELDRIDGE CLEAVER (1935–1998) — Writer, activist, Black Panther Party member.

PETER CLIFTON (UNKNOWN) — Former slave from
Winnsboro, South Carolina. His account of his experiences
as a slave recorded during the 1930s by the Federal Writers
Project of the WPA.

JOHNNIE L. COCHRAN, JR. (1937–2005) — Lawyer, writer.

NAT "KING" COLE (1919–1965) — Singer, jazz pianist, actor,
activist, winner of Grammy Lifetime Achievement Award,
Down Beat Jazz Hall of Fame inductee, Hit Parade Hall of
Fame inductee.

MARVA COLLINS (B. 1936) — Educator, reformer, recipient of
National Humanities Medal for her work in education reform.

JAMES CONE (B. 1938) — Scholar, writer, theologian.

BILL COSBY (B. 1937) — Comedian, actor, writer, television
producer, activist, Emmy Award winner, Grammy Award
winner, Presidential Medal of Freedom recipient.

BENJAMIN DAVIS, JR. (1877–1970) — First African American
general in the U.S. Army.

OSSIE DAVIS (1917–2005) — Actor, writer, director, activist,
Grammy Award winner, Kennedy Center Honoree.

SAMMY DAVIS, JR., (1925–1990) — Dancer, singer, musician,
comedian, winner of Grammy, Emmy, and Tony Awards,
Grammy Hall of Fame inductee, Grammy Lifetime
Achievement Award recipient, and Kennedy Center honoree.

A. ELIZABETH DELANY (1891–1995) AND SARAH LOUISE DELANY (1889–1999) — The Delany sisters (a doctor of dental surgery and an educator, respectively) knew many artists from the Harlem Renaissance, and wrote the best-selling *Having Our Say* about their century-long lives.

DAVID DINKINS (B. 1927) — Lawyer, politician, first black mayor of New York City from 1990 to 1994.

FREDERICK DOUGLASS (1818–1895) — Escaped slave who rose to national prominence as a brilliant orator, writer, and editor. Leader in the Abolitionist movement, consultant to Abraham Lincoln, Minister to Haiti from 1889 to 1891.

RITA DOVE (B. 1952) — Writer of poetry and short stories, winner of Pulitzer Prize for poetry in 1987 for *Thomas and Beulah*. Chosen as poet laureate to Library of Congress in 1993, professor at University of Virginia.

W. E. B. DU BOIS (1868–1963) — Scholar, sociologist, educator, writer, leading African American intellectual of his day and founder of the NAACP.

MICHAEL ERIC DYSON (B. 1958) — Scholar, minister, writer, professor, radio host.

MARIAN WRIGHT EDELMAN (B. 1939) — Lawyer, civil rights activist, writer, founder and president of Children's Defense Fund.

DUKE ELLINGTON (1899–1974) — Composer, pianist, bandleader, Grammy Award winner, Grammy Lifetime Achievement Award winner, Songwriters Hall of Fame inductee, Presidential Medal of Freedom recipient.

RALPH ELLISON (1914–1994) — Scholar, educator, writer, best known for his landmark novel *Invisible Man*, which won the National Book Award in 1953.

LOUIS FARRAKHAN (B. 1933) — Principal minister for the Nation of Islam, advocate, activist known for his controversial oratory.

ELLA FITZGERALD (1917–1996) — Singer, songwriter, bandleader, actress, Grammy Award winner, Grammy Lifetime Achievement Award winner, Presidential Medal of Freedom recipient, U.S. National Medal of Arts Recipient, Kennedy Center honoree.

ROBERTA FLACK (B. 1937) — Singer-songwriter, pianist, musician, winner of multiple Grammy Awards.

ARETHA FRANKLIN (B. 1942) — Singer, songwriter, pianist, multiple Grammy Award winner, Presidential Medal of Freedom recipient, Rock and Roll Hall of Fame inductee.

JOHN HOPE FRANKLIN (1915–2009) — Scholar, writer, historian, professor, Presidential Medal of Freedom recipient.

MORGAN FREEMAN (B. 1937) — Actor, director, narrator, winner of Academy Award, Golden Globe, SAG Award, and Kennedy Center honoree.

AMY GARVEY (1895–1973) — Journalist, editor, publisher, wife of Marcus Garvey.

MARCUS GARVEY (1887–1940) — Orator, writer, organizer of first major U.S. black nationalist movement.

HENRY LOUIS GATES, JR. (B. 1950) — Scholar, professor, writer, chairman of Afro-American Studies at Harvard.

ALTHEA GIBSON (1927–2003) — Tennis player, first African American women to win a Grand Slam title, Tennis Hall of Fame inductee.

BOB GIBSON (B. 1935) — Baseball player, Cy Young Award winner, won two World Series titles with St. Louis Cardinals in 1964, 1967. National Baseball Hall of Fame inductee.

NIKKI GIOVANNI (B. 1943) — Writer of poetry and prose, activist, educator.

DANNY GLOVER (B. 1946) — Actor, director, activist.

WHOOPI GOLDBERG (B. 1955) — Actress, comedian, talk show host, writer, media personality, activist. Winner of Academy, Grammy, Tony, Emmy, and Day Time Emmy Awards. Kennedy Center honoree receiving Mark Twain Prize for American Humor.

BERRY GORDY (B. 1929) — Music producer, founder of Motown Records, Rock and Roll Hall of Fame inductee.

ELIJAH GREEN (UNKNOWN) — Former slave from Charleston, South Carolina. His account of his experiences as a slave recorded during the 1930s by the Federal Writers Project of the WPA.

BRYANT GUMBEL (B. 1948) — Television journalist, sports and newscaster, sports anchor, winner of multiple Emmy Awards.

LORRAINE HANSBERRY (1930–1965) — Playwright, activist. Her play *A Raisin in the Sun* was the first drama written by an African American woman to be made into a Broadway production. The play went on to win the New York Drama Critics Circle Award.

JIMI HENDRIX (1942–1970) — Guitarist, singer, songwriter, Grammy Lifetime Achievement Award winner, Rock and Roll Hall of Fame inductee.

BILLIE HOLIDAY (1915–1959) — Jazz singer, songwriter, Grammy Lifetime Achievement Award winner, Rock and Roll Hall of Fame inductee, Blues Hall of Fame inductee.

BENJAMIN L. HOOKS (B. 1925) — Lawyer, minister, executive director of NAACP from 1977 to 1992.

LENA HORNE (B. 1917) — Singer, dancer, actress, social activist. First African American studio contract performer, winner of multiple Grammy Awards, Kennedy Center Honoree.

MILDRED HOWARD (B. 1945) — Prolific mixed media and installation artist.

LANGSTON HUGHES (1902–1967) — Journalist and writer of poetry, novels, and non-fiction. He was a leading figure in the Harlem Renaissance.

ZORA NEALE HURSTON (1891–1960) — Writer, active in the Harlem Renaissance.

ICE-T (B. 1958) — Hip-hop artist, actor, writer, Grammy Award winner.

JESSE JACKSON (B. 1941) — Minister, civil rights activist, political activist, presidential candidate in 1984 and 1988, Presidential Medal of Freedom recipient.

MAHALIA JACKSON (1912–1972) — Gospel singer, actress, winner of multiple Grammy Awards, inductee to Grammy Hall of Fame.

MICHAEL JACKSON (1958–2009) — Singer, recording artist, dancer, entertainer, innovator, humanitarian. Winner of 13 Grammy Awards, Two-time inductee to Rock and Roll Hall of Fame, Holds Guinness World Record for The Most Successful Entertainer of All Time. He donated millions of dollars to charities the world over much of it through his Heal the World Foundation.

JOHN E. JACOB (B. 1934) — Civil rights leader, president of the National Urban League.

HARRIET JACOBS (1813–1897) — Escaped slave who wrote an autobiographical account of her years in slavery entitled *Incidents in the Life of a Slave Girl*, which was published under the pseudonym Linda Brent.

JAY-Z (B. 1969) — Hip-hop artist, songwriter, record producer, record executive, Grammy Award winner.

DEREK JETER (B. 1974) — Baseball player and captain of the New York Yankees with whom he has won four World Series to date.

JAMES EARL JONES (B. 1931) — Actor, writer, Emmy Award winner, Tony Award winner, Grammy Award winner, National Medal of Arts recipient, Kennedy Center honoree, Theater Hall of Fame inductee.

QUINCY JONES (B. 1933) — Record producer, music conductor and arranger, film composer, musician, won twenty-seven Grammys including a Grammy Legend Award.

BARBARA C. JORDAN (1936–1996) — U.S. House of Representative from Texas, Presidential Medal of Freedom recipient.

JUNE JORDAN (1936–2002) — Caribbean-American writer, educator, activist.

MICHAEL JORDAN (B. 1963) — Basketball player, businessman, writer. He led the Chicago Bulls to three straight national championships and three subsequent championships. He's the winner of two Olympic Gold medals, and an inductee to the Basketball Hall of Fame.

JOHN O. KILLENS (1916–1987) — Writer, professor.

MARTIN LUTHER KING, JR. (1929–1968) — Baptist minister, prominent leader of mass civil rights movement in the U.S. from 1950s until his assassination in 1968. Founder and first president of Southern Christian Leadership Conference (1957), awarded Nobel Peace Prize (1964). Posthumously awarded the Presidential Medal of Freedom and the Congressional Gold Medal. In 1986, Martin Luther King, Jr., Day was made a U.S. national holiday.

GLADYS KNIGHT (B. 1944) — Singer, songwriter, actress, winner of multiple Grammy Awards.

LENNY KRAVITZ (B. 1964) — Singer, songwriter, instrumentalist, record producer, arranger, winner of multiple Grammy Awards.

LL COOL J (B. 1968) — Hip-hop artist, actor, writer, winner of multiple Grammy Awards.

SARA LAWRENCE-LIGHTFOOT (B. 1944) — Scholar, sociologist, educator, writer.

SPIKE LEE (B. 1957) — Director, producer, writer, actor, professor, Emmy Award winner.

JULIUS LESTER (B. 1939) — Folk musician, writer, activist, educator.

ABBEY LINCOLN (B. 1930) — Jazz singer, songwriter, actress.

ALAIN LOCKE (1885–1954) — Writer, philosopher, educator, considered the father of the Harlem Renaissance.

AUDRE LORDE (1934–1992) — Caribbean-born American writer, poet, activist.

JOE LOUIS (1914–1981) — Heavyweight boxing champion, Congressional Gold Medal recipient, International Boxing Hall of Fame inductee.

JOHN LOVELL, JR. (1907–1974) — Writer.

JOSEPH LOWERY (B. 1921) — Minister, civil rights activist.

BERNIE MAC (1957–2008) — Actor, comedian, Emmy Award winner.

CLAUDE MCKAY (1890–1948) — Jamaican-born American writer, early and most militant writer of the Harlem Renaissance.

RONALD MCNAIR (1950–1986) — NASA Astronaut, physicist, died during the launching of the Space Shuttle *Discovery*, Congressional Space Medal of Honor recipient.

MALCOLM X (1925–1965) — Religious leader. He converted to Islam while in prison at the age of twenty-five and subsequently became a highly influential minister for the Nation of Islam. He advocated black nationalism and separatism. After his break with Elijah Muhammad, he founded Muslim Mosque, Inc. (1964). He was assassinated in Harlem. His seminal autobiography was published posthumously in 1965.

THURGOOD MARSHALL (1908–1993) — Jurist who was the first African American to be appointed to the U.S. Supreme Court (1967). While on the Court, he was a champion of individual and First Amendment rights. He retired in 1991.

KELLY MILLER (1863–1939) — Mathematician, sociologist, writer, journalist.

TONI MORRISON (B. 1931) — Writer of novels, short stories, plays, and non-fiction. Winner of the American Book Award for *The Song of Solomon*, the Pulitzer Prize for fiction for *Beloved*, and in 1993 she became the first African American woman to receive the Nobel Prize for literature. She has taught at universities including Yale, SUNY, and Princeton.

CAROL MOSELEY-BRAUN (B. 1947) — Lawyer, first black woman to be seated in the U.S. Senate (1992).

ELIJAH MUHAMMAD (1897–1975) — Leader of the Nation of Islam, civil rights activist.

EDDIE MURPHY (B. 1961) — Actor, director, producer, comedian, singer. Winner of SAG Award and Golden Globe Award.

BARACK OBAMA (B. 1961) — Lawyer, writer, community organizer, state senator, U.S. Senator, forty-fourth President of the United States.

JESSE OWENS (1913–1980) — Track and field athlete, writer, four-time gold medal Olympiad, Congressional Gold Medal recipient, Presidential Medal of Freedom recipient.

ABOUT THE CONTRIBUTORS

SATCHEL PAIGE (1906–1982) — Legendary baseball player who played for several teams in the Negro Leagues before entering the major leagues in 1948. He helped the Cleveland Indians to a World Series victory in 1948 and in 1971 he was inducted into the National Baseball Hall of Fame.

CHARLIE PARKER (1920–1955) — Jazz saxophonist, composer, Grammy Lifetime Achievement Award winner.

GORDON PARKS (1912–2006) — Photographer, writer, musician, composer, director, National Medal of Arts Recipient.

ROSA PARKS (1913–2005) — Civil rights activist and NAACP organizer whose refusal to give up her seat on a Montgomery bus on December 1, 1955 helped to begin the Montgomery bus boycott which first brought national attention to Martin Luther King, Jr. She continued to work for social reform, wrote several books, and received many honors and awards including the Presidential Medal of Freedom and the Congressional Gold Medal.

ANN PERRY (UNKNOWN) — Former slave from Charleston, South Carolina. Her account of her experiences as a slave recorded during the 1930s by the Federal Writers Project of the WPA.

WILLIAM PICKENS (1881–1954) — Scholar, dean, writer, field secretary for NAACP for more than twenty years.

ANN PLATO (1820–?) — Writer, educator.

SIDNEY POITIER (B. 1927) — Actor, director, writer, diplomat. Winner of Academy Award, Golden Globe, Grammy, SAG Lifetime Achievement Award, AFI Lifetime Achievement Award, Kennedy Center honoree. He was the first African American man to win an Oscar (Best Actor for *Lilies of the Field*, 1963).

ADAM CLAYTON POWELL, JR. (1908–1972) — Pastor of Harlem's Abyssinian Baptist Church from 1937 to 1971, first African American member of New York City Council, eleven-term member U.S. House of Representatives.

COLIN POWELL (B. 1937) — Four-star General, U.S. National Security Advisor, Chairman of the Joint Chiefs of Staff, U.S. Secretary of State. First African American to serve on Joint Chiefs of Staff and first African American Secretary of State.

LEONTYNE PRICE (B. 1927) — Operatic soprano, winner of nineteen Grammy Awards, recipient of Presidential Medal of Freedom, National Medal of Arts, and Kennedy Center Honoree.

RICHARD PRYOR (1940–2005) — Comedian, actor, writer, considered one of the most influential stand-up comedians of all time. Posthumously awarded Grammy Lifetime Achievement Award.

PUBLIC ENEMY — Influential and politically active 1980's hip-hop group led by Chuck D and Favor Flav.

QUEEN LATIFAH (B. 1970) — Hip-hop artist, model, actress, winner of Golden Globe, SAG, and Grammy Awards.

ROBIN QUIVERS (B. 1952) — Radio talk show personality, actress, writer.

A. PHILLIP RANDOLPH (1889–1979) — Civil rights leader, union organizer.

CONDALEEZA RICE (B. 1954) — Scholar, professor, diplomat, U.S. National Security Advisor, U.S. Secretary of State. First woman to serve as National Security Advisor and first African American woman to serve as Secretary of State.

PAUL ROBESON (1898–1976) — Athlete, lawyer, scholar, actor, singer, social and labor activist. College Football Hall of Fame inductee, Lifetime Grammy Award winner.

BILL "BOJANGLES" ROBINSON (1878–1949) — Dancer, actor.

JACKIE ROBINSON (1919–1972) — Baseball player and first African American to play in Major League Baseball (1947). He won one World Series with the Brooklyn Dodgers. He was the first black player to be elected to the National Baseball Hall of Fame and is the recipient of the Congressional Gold Medal and Presidential Medal of Freedom.

WILMA RUDOLPH (1940–1994) — Track and field athlete, first U.S. woman to win three gold medals during track and field in a single Olympics game.

BILL RUSSELL (B. 1934) — Basketball player who led the Boston Celtics to eleven NBA Championships, U.S. Gold Medal Olympiad, Basketball Hall of Fame inductee, Presidential Medal of Freedom recipient.

THE SCOTTSBORO BOYS — Nine young African American men who were arrested and charged with raping two white women in 1931. After cursory trials with no effective representation, all defendants were found guilty and sentenced to death. Though the Supreme Court ruled the defendants' due process had been denied and overturned the death penalties, the cases were retried in state court and five of the nine defendants were falsely convicted and served between six and nineteen years in prison.

AL SHARPTON (B. 1954) — Minister, social justice activist.

RUSSELL SIMMONS (B. 1957) — Entrepreneur, co-founder of Def Jam Records, record producer, clothing line creator, activist, writer.

WILL SMITH (B. 1968) — Actor, film producer, rapper, winner of multiple Grammys.

DOROTHY S. STRICKLAND (B. 1933) — Professor, writer.

CLARENCE THOMAS (B. 1948) — U.S. Supreme Court Justice. He is the second African American to serve on the Court after Thurgood Marshall.

HOWARD THURMAN (1899–1981) — Scholar, writer, orator, educator, theologian.

JOHNNIE TILLMON (B. 1926) — Founding chairperson and subsequent director of the National Welfare Rights Organization.

JEAN TOOMER (1894–1967) — Writer, active in Harlem Renaissance.

SOJOURNER TRUTH (C. 1797–1883) — Abolitionist, women's rights activist, worked for Union cause during the Civil War, lectured in more than twenty states for African American and women's rights.

HARRIET TUBMAN (C. 1820–1913) — Escaped slave turned abolitionist, women's suffragist, and Union scout and spy during the Civil War. She used the Underground Railroad to bring approximately 300 slaves to freedom.

NAT TURNER (1800–1831) — Led armed slave revolt in August of 1831. After his capture, he gave his famous "Confessions of Nat Turner," and was hanged in November of 1831.

WATERS E. TURPIN (1910–1968) — Scholar, writer, professor.

ALICE WALKER (B. 1944) — Writer, winner of the Pulitzer Prize for fiction for *The Color Purple*.

MARGARET WALKER (1915–1998) — Educator and writer of poetry, essays, and novels. A leading poet of her era, her volume *For My People* won the Yale Younger Poets Award in 1942.

FATS WALLER (1904–1943) — Pianist, singer, composer, songwriter, Grammy Lifetime Achievement Award winner, Songwriters Hall of Fame inductee.

BOOKER T. WASHINGTON (1856–1915) — Educator, writer, most prominent African American leader of his time, first president of Tuskegee Institute, advisor to presidents Theodore Roosevelt and William Howard Taft on matters of race.

DENZEL WASHINGTON (B. 1954) — Actor, director, producer, Academy Award winner, Golden Globe Winner.

FAYE WATTLETON (B. 1943) — Educator, women's rights activist, president of Planned Parenthood.

IDA B. WELLS (1862–1931) — Journalist, editor, suffragist, civil rights activist.

CORNEL WEST (B. 1953) — Minister, professor, writer, civil rights activist.

JOHN A. WILLIAMS (B. 1925) — Writer, journalist, professor.

VANESSA WILLIAMS (B. 1963) — Singer, songwriter, actress, activist. First African American woman to be crowned Miss America.

AUGUST WILSON, JR. (1945–2005) — Playwright, two time winner of the Pulitzer Prize for fiction for *Fences* and *The Piano Lesson*, Tony Award for Best Play for *Fences*.

OPRAH WINFREY (B. 1952) — Talk show icon, writer, producer, actress, philanthropist, humanitarian, activist, publisher. She was once ranked as the only African American billionaire and currently ranked as the most philanthropic African American in history.

STEVIE WONDER (B. 1950) — Singer, songwriter, instrumentalist, producer, activist. He's won twenty-two Grammy Awards, Grammy Lifetime Achievement Award, Academy Award, Rock and Roll Hall of Fame inductee, Songwriters Hall of Fame inductee, Kennedy Center honoree.

TIGER WOODS (B. 1975) — Golfer, whose career to date ranks him among the best players of all time. He has won fourteen professional major golf championships, sixty-six PGA tour events, and thirty-six European Tour wins. He is the first person of African American descent to win the Masters Tournament.

CARTER G. WOODSON (1875–1950) — Scholar, writer, founder, historian, organizer of Negro History Week (1926), which evolved into Black History Month in 1976.

RICHARD WRIGHT (1908–1960) — Writer of novels, poetry, essays, and short stories, best known for his 1940 novel *Native Son*. He is considered one of the most important writers of the twentieth century.

ANDREW YOUNG (B. 1932) — U.S. House of Representatives from Georgia, Mayor of Atlanta, U.S. Ambassador to the United Nations, pastor, civil rights activist.